AF538704

MENTALLY HANDICAPPED CHILDREN AND FAMILY STRESS

Mentally Handicapped Children and Family Stress

M. Annapurna
Deptt. of Home Science
S.V. University
Tirupati (A.P.)

DISCOVERY PUBLISHING HOUSE
NEW DELHI—110 002

Reprinted - 2019

First Published - 1999

ISBN: 978-81-7141-395-9

Mentally Handicapped Children and Family Stress

Published by:

DISCOVERY PUBLISHING HOUSE PVT. LTD.

4383/4B, Ansari Road, Darya Ganj
New Delhi-110 002 (India)
Phone: +91-11-23279245, 43596064-65
Fax: +91-11-23253475
E-mail: discoverypublishinghouse@gmail.com
sales@discoverypublishinggroup.com
web: www.discoverypublishinggroup.com

Printed at:
Infinity Imaging Systems
Delhi

Foreword

From time immemorial, family has played a crucial role in the development of child. Parents particularly play dominant role in shaping the personality of the individual. The family comes under stress when the child has special needs due to the condition of mental retardation. Although rearing practices may not be different in the case of special child vis-a-vis a normal child, yet the family undergoes hardships due to the condition of mental retardation. When the condition is severe, the parents are burdened with care and management including taking care of toilet, grooming and self-care needs. Normal children grow up to become independent whereas the child with mental retardation continue to remain dependent upon parents.

Parents have the need to find out more about the condition of mental retardation and get the right direction in understanding the nature and causation of the problem. Occasionally parents are confronted with the problem whether to go in for a second child and if so what are the chances that the second child will also have mental retardation. With the child having mental retardation continue to remain at home, the socialisation of the family gets restricted. In view of the above, the families are definitely under stress and the social scientists and educators have important role to help families cope up with the situation.

Dr. M. Annapurna for her doctoral dissertation chose the problem of finding stressful effects on family in rearing and managing mentally handicapped children. She took a sample of 60 families from Chandragiri Mandal in Chittoor District and information was collected on family resources, coping, functioning, integration, burden, satisfaction and problem behaviours in children with mental retardation. The age group of children with mental retardation chosen for inclusion in the study was 6–18 years which represented childhood, late childhood and adolescence. Interviews were carried out with 60 fathers, 60 mothers and 60 significant other persons in the family predominantly grandparents and siblings.

All the three groups experienced burden on the family, perceived disruption in the family functioning, lowered family satisfaction and perceived behaviour problems affecting the family life. Relative contribution of independent variables studied through regression analysis gave relationship between different variables and the contribution to each variable towards the depending variable.

The research work carried out by Dr. M. Annapurna is a step further on the building blocks of our understanding the families having a child with mental retardation. It is hoped that the understanding obtained will help us in planning a programme for families in order to reduce the stress and enhance their coping capabilities. It is an excellent work and should be read by all serious thinkers in the file of social sciences who have devoted their time and energy to understand family and its role towards persons with mental retardation.

Dr. D.K. Menon
Director, NIMH

Acknowledgements

I deem it a great pleasure to acknowledge my profound gratitude to my research supervisor Dr. V.V. Bharathi, Reader in Home Science, S.V. University for her able guidance, valuable suggestions and instant help given to me. She was a real good friend, a philosopher and a guide in the truest sense. Her uninterrupted encouragement, keen interest and personal warmth have been a source of motivation to me throughout the course of this study. I am highly indebted to her.

It is with immense pleasure I take this opportunity to express my deep sense of gratitude to Prof. S.R. Venkatramaiah, Retired Professor of Clinical Psychology, Department of Home Science, S.V. University for his constructive criticism and valuable ideas. His suggestions in critical times helped me to move forward in my research work.

My sincere thanks and appreciation are due to Dr. S. Padmanabhaiah, Reader and Head of the Department of Education, S.V. University for his skillful guidance in the statistical analysis, without whose help this work would not have taken this shape.

I profoundly thank Dr. V. Sreedevi, Reader, Department of Home Science, S.V. University for the sincere help and encouragement throughout the course of research.

I express my sincere and heartfelt gratitude to Prof. E. Satyanarayana, Department of Statistics, S.V. University for the valuable suggestions not only in statistical part but at crucial times during my research work.

I am highly grateful to Dr. Sujatha Ramamoorthy, Reader and Head of the Department of Home Science, S.V. University for providing me facilities throughout my research work.

I am thankful to Dr. V. Kodandarami Reddy, Reader, Department of Econometrics, S.V. University, who was co-operative in coining computer programmes for analysis and could complete the work diligently in required time.

I owe my thanks to Ms. Gayathri, Teaching Assistant, Department of Home Science, S.V. University, who helped me in coding and tabulation work.

I thank Sri S.H.K. Reddy, Librarian, NIMH, for his valuable service in procuring relevant literature for the study.

I am immensely grateful to all the respondents who extended their whole hearted co-operation in providing the necessary information.

My appreciation and thanks are due to Mr. K. Prahlada Rao, for typing the thesis without any trouble.

M. Annapurna

Contents

1
Introduction

Accepting a child with mental handicap becomes difficult to parents and the whole family particularly when competence and achievement are very much valued in modern world. Thus when it suddenly becomes necessary for parents to love someone who has a very limited capacity the parents are put in conflicting situation and result in a great deal of stress.

Olshansky (1962) has speculated that almost all parents who have a mentally retarded child suffer from chronic sorrow throughout their lives. The extent of this sorrow may differ from one parent to another but most will have manifestation of sorrow in varying degrees.

The effects of rearing a handicapped child on the family appear to be complex. Many studies and personal observations agree that the families are faced with many problems including those of management, finance, deprivation of rest and leisure to the parents. Some families may cope very well and remain cohesive and creative units in which other children may grow up normally and happily. But some families may get over strained by the presence of handicapped child and eventually disintegrate. What makes the difference ? Is it the material resources which facilitate family functioning in spite of the stressful effects of having a handicapped child ? Is it the social support the family receives, which will enhance family functioning ? Answers to these puzzling questions need to be explored.

The birth and continuing care of mentally retarded children are often stressful experiences for family members as these children's difficulties inevitably touch the lives of those around them (Crnic, Friedrich, Greenberg, 1983 and Featherstone, 1980). The effects on the family unit can be far reaching, restrictive and disruptive and they may be economic, social or emotional (Schonell and Watts, 1957). Consequently, parents of retarded children have generally been viewed as being "at-risk" for a variety of family life problems and emotional difficulties. Paramount among their family life problems are unusual care giving demands and restrictive time demands (Beckman, 1983). For many family members especially mothers, management of daily needs of retarded child may constitute an all time consuming task (Bradshaw and Lawton, 1978; Butler, Gill, Pomeroy and Fartrell, 1978).

Crnic and Greenberg (1985) found that the cumulative impact of daily parenting hassles and difficulties in dealing with children represent significant stressors that may subsequently affect parent and family functioning.

In addition, families often face increased financial burdens (Holroyed, 1974); McAndrew, 1976; Richards and McIntosh, 1973). At the same time family income may get reduced because care giving responsibilities make it difficult for two parents to work out side the home.

An added area of concern for some families is difficulty in managing family relationships (Featherstone, 1980; Friedrich and Friedrich, 1981; and Gath, 1977). Roles within the family may need to be restructured (Farber, 1960; Kazak and Marvin, 1984) and the resulting strain may manifest itself in family problems including high rates of desertion, divorce, family quarreling and marital breakdown (Gath, 1977; Holt, 1958 and Reed and Reed, 1965).

Available literature suggests that not only the parents but the families with handicapped children are at-risk for numerous difficulties (Bristol, Schopler and McConnanghey 1984; DeMayer, 1979; Tew, Payne and Lawrence, 1974). But in spite of such high risk status some parents report that they adapt successfully to the stresses that are chronic and periodically extreme (Akerley, 1975). Outcomes reports of successful functioning in families with a child who has handicaps are inconsistent. One explanation for such inconsistent research findings is that a family's reaction to stress is highly variable ranging from healthy adaptation to mal adaptation. Such variation in response is explained by more recent models of family adaptation to stress such as McCubbin and Patterson's (1982-83) Double ABCX or Family Adjustment and Adaptation Response (FAAR) model and Crnic, Friedrich and Greenberg's (1983) Adaptation model for families, with children who have mental retardation, that highlight the role of coping behaviour in mediating the impact of stress. Such models suggest that stress can indeed result in family distress but also allow the possibility that stress may result in more sophisticated family functioning if resources are sufficient.

According to Goldie (1966) for these parents, the handicapped child is the living grave of their hope for a normal baby. The initial response of parents is most vividly described by parents themselves as grief (Brinkworth, 1970). Solnit and Stark (1961) regard the grief of parents with a handicapped child as similar to that following bereavement and they suggest that the experience of mourning is necessary before a healthy adjustment can be made, yet unlike a death in the family the birth of an abnormal baby means that the parents are constantly reminded of their sorrow by the child's continued presence. When the parents' expectations of a healthy normal child are contradicted by the birth of a handicapped one, their coping mechanisms are severely put to test.

The effect of a handicapped child on the stability of the family unit has been the subject of considerable comment and research. Farber (1960) and Fatheringham et al., (1971) strongly opined that the severely retarded child's presence impedes the family development and places significant stress on the family unit.

The birth of handicapped child places the family in a cultural dilemma. Society views parenthood positively but it views parenthood of a handicapped child negatively (Zuk, 1962).

Many parents report that the uncertainty of their mentally handicapped child's future caused the family deep concern and stress. According to Wikler (1981) a social-work researcher, the retarded child is a chronic stress to the family. This chronic stress gets "recycled" at each juncture of the life span when a developmental step would normally occur in the affected person. For example, when a retarded child reaches the age of high school graduation and cannot be graduated and launched as normal children are, the family is newly reminded of the hopelessness of the child's situation.

Added to them, grandparents often experience a duel grief, a mounting for the loss of an expected grandchild who would carry on the family tradition and a sorrow for the life long burden and reduced opportunities, their own child faces in raising this grandchild. The support of a grandparent, a sibling, an aunt, an uncle can be extremely important to the handicapped child and the parents (Schell, 1981) when those relatives do not seem to understand or enter into a supportive role their reactions to the child can be extremely painful for parents (Ferris, 1980).

The stigma of the handicapped person is one of shame and inferiority (Wright, 1960) which marks the person as tinted and discounted (Goffman, 1963). For many handicapped individuals and their families the most devastating consequences of being handicapped are often not the direct physical or mental results of impairment itself, but rather the attitudes and reactions of those in the society, who are not handicapped.

Parents' belief in possible "Cure" is usually reflected by the unfortunate and wasteful tendency of parents who are unwilling or unable to accept the inevitable limitations and continually travel from place to place seeking a cure. The parental anxiety only disturbs the child and affects the family life since unnecessary and wasteful expenses are heavy drain on the family resources.

The parents' unrealistic expectation that sooner or later the child would start functioning like any other person with normal intelligence probably arises from their excessive hopefulness and a conscious or unconscious wish that the child may get cured and will function like any other normal child.

Another area in which data would be needed is in the context of a study of needs, concerns, coping mechanisms within families and the objective and subjective burden placed on families by the presence of a retarded person.

The system of joint families in developing countries is said to provide a network of support for handicapped and impaired persons, but the existing data appear to invalidate such belief. (Mia et al., 1979; Gupta and Sethi, 1970).

Sell (1984) stated that the presence of a retarded child or adult in the family may pose a serious threat to the cohesion of extended families, especially in rural societies.

A recent publication from Norway by Ingstad and Sommerchild (1983) dealt with families with a handicapped child (not only with mental retardation but also children with other chronic diseases). They described the large variations in how a family reacted. Some families eventually found a way of coping and compensating both for the extra demands of the handicapped and for the needs of the other family members. Other families, however, were not able to find a solution of their own and so depended on outside help. Analysis of qualitative data showed how the past created important constraints and possibilities for coping in the present situation. For those who represented the strongest and the weakest forms of coping, it was possible to identify "good" and "bad" coping styles.

All the factors so far discussed may directly/indirectly affect the functioning of family. It may be more so in the rural set up which is markedly different by its large percentage of illiterate poor population, who are helpless and unaware of the causes of mental handicap and the agencies that render help. Present study is expected to throw some light on perceptions of parents and other family members about the stressful effects caused by the presence of a mentally handicapped child.

Review of Relevant Literature

The available literature of research presented in this chapter are classified and reviewed under the following heads. They are :

1. Studies related to problems faced by the parents of mentally handicapped children.

2. Studies related to family stress with a mentally handicapped child.

3. Studies related to the influence of mentally handicapped child on family functioning.

4. Studies related to support systems for the families with mentally handicapped children.

Studies Related to Problems Faced by the Parents of Mentally Handicapped Children

Studies on the effects on parents caring for a subnormal child have yielded conflicting results. Some investigators have indicated that the responsibility of rearing a subnormal child may be detrimental to the health and happiness of the mother. As long back as 1957, Schonell and Watts described the effects of mentally handicapped children on the family unit as far reaching, restrictive and disruptive and they may be economic, social or emotional. They conducted a study on fifty (50) Australian families with subnormal children. The mother's mental health was described as being in 'constant jeopardy' and the social interactions normally involved in shopping or taking a holiday was severely limited.

Holt (1957) studied two hundred and seven (207) families with a subnormal child living at home in Sheffield found that nineteen per cent (19%) of the mothers were exhausted by the physical work and emotional stress involved. Fathers were said to suffer to a lesser degree, but marriages were strained by parental quarreling.

In 1960, Caldwell and Gaze introduced a control group by comparing families with subnormal children living at home with those of comparable children living in an institution. The results indicated no significant difference between the mothers of institutionalized and non-institutionalized children. Contrary to those results Tizard and Grad (1961) found that families with a subnormal child at home were dominated by the "burden of care" while those with a child in an institution were able to lead nearly normal lives.

Farber's (1962) classic studies conducted in the late 1950s and early 1960s on the effect of a handicapped child on the stability of the family unit need special mention in family research.

Farber studied two hundred and forty (240) families with severely retarded children (I.Q. of 50 or below) who were 16 years of age or under. One hundred and seventy five families of the 240 had a retarded child at home and sixty five had placed their children in an institution. A two and half hour interview of the parents was conducted in the home. In addition parents were asked to complete a series of scales and questionnaires and the family's marital integration was also measured. Thus the subjects were scrutinized rather intensively which makes Farber's research one of the most important in this area.

However, Ross (1964) points out that data were not based on comparisons between family integration before and after placement of the child in an institution, which constitutes a weakness in the study and leaves unresolved question of whether better marital integration was achieved as a result of the decision to institutionalize the child or whether other factors are operating.

The results of Farber's studies indicated the following :

1. Marriages were more adversely affected when the retarded child was kept at home only when the child was a boy. This finding was more pronounced in lower than in middle class families.
2. Normal brothers were adversely affected by the institutionalization of the retarded sibling.
3. Normal sisters showed more personality problems when the retarded sibling was in the home than when he was in an institution whether the institutionalized child was a boy or girl.
4. Emotional support available to the mother outside the immediate family appears to have a positive effect on marital integration especially when the wife had frequent interaction with her own mother.
5. Beneficial effects of placing the retarded son in an institution were found among non-Catholics but not among Catholic families. Non-Catholics suffered more marital discord when the retarded boy was at home.

Farber (1959) concluded that the parent can expect that a retarded boy especially after the age of nine will probably have a disruptive effect on marital relations; he can anticipate personality problems for the sister, who is given many responsibilities of the child; the parent must be aware of the degree to which the family has its own resources and supportive interaction in facing crisis situations and he can expect the degree of helplessness of the retarded to affect the personality of his normal children adversely.

Subsequent studies by Farber (1962) revealed that :

1. Normal brothers and sisters who had sustained interaction with their retarded siblings professed such life goals as (a) devotion to a worthwhile cause and (b) making a contribution to the mankind.

Normal siblings come to regard sustained interaction with retarded siblings as a duty and in turn seemed to select life careers which require dedication and sacrifice in the service of mankind.

2. Families with a child-oriented, home-oriented or parent-oriented philosophy were more integrated than those lacking a consistent orientation whether the child was at home or in an institution.

   Farber's studies reinforce the notion that parents of handicapped children must be viewed in the context of a variety of interacting factors.

Using a battery of self administered tests, Cummings, et al., (1966) compared mothers of mentally retarded children with those of chronically ill children and concluded that the former group were subjected to greater psychological stress in day-to-day management.

Hammer and Barnard (1966) reported that emotional disorders are another complication with the retarded. The impairment of reasoning abilities reduces the child's adaptive capacities adding emotional stress within the family. The mentally retarded child will tend to misinterpret and over-react to ordinary stimuli and such behaviour contributes to his limited tolerance to stress. The adolescent retarded when he does not behave to his age, he is reprimanded and asked to behave like an adult even though his mental age might be that of a 7 year old. The problems become compounded by society's lack of acceptance of immature behaviour by the physically large child. Parents and siblings are embarrassed when confronted repeatedly by stressful situations that are more difficult to control in the older retarded child.

Parents often identify with their handicapped Child's emotions to the point of feeling personally responsible for the child's failures.

They also reported that the most frequent complaints from the family and school personnel involving the moderately retarded males were those of masturbation, genital exposure and overtly affectionate behaviour, whereas the moderately retarded females presented problems with respect to caring for their menstrual periods and to masturbation.

Wolfensberger's model of three crises is helpful in understanding the difficulties of individual families with a subnormal child (Wolfensberger, 1968). From a survey of Mongol children in the Oxford region, there is an over representation of children from social classes I and V who are admitted to the sub-normality hospitals at an early age. The factors that make the burden of a subnormal child intolerable are unlikely to be the same for families at the extremes of the social ladder. Social class I families esteem highly those standards of education and behaviour that have enabled them to succeed. Therefore, for such families the value crises is the most poignant and they are deeply distressed by the fact that their child can never aspire to what they themselves hold dear.

In contrast the value crisis is less threatening to those whose attainments are modest. Instead they fixed themselves overburdened by the necessary extra expenditure caused by the heavy wear and tear on clothes or household decorations by subnormal child (Younghusband et al., 1970). They are also unable to pay for help which can make the reality crisis less formidable for more affluent families.

A less extensive yet major study was carried out in Toronto by Fatheringham et al., (1971). The investigators hypothesized that living with a severely retarded child would be difficult to endure and therefore the family would be subjected to stress, the degree of which would be influenced by the characteristics of the child, the family's capacity for coping and the available community support. The study examined the consequences on the family of severely retarded children who were either institutionalized or remained at home.

The general results of the study did not indicate significantly different changes in the functioning levels of the retarded children in the two different living situations (home and institution) over the one year period. The proportion of institutionalized families showing improvement was greater than that of community families and the greatest decrease in functioning in the later was observed in the siblings' and parents' adequacy in caring for the retarded child.

Farber's and Fatheringham's studies taken together strongly suggest that the severely retarded child's presence impedes the family development and places significant stress on the family unit.

Farber reflects on the sociological and psychological ramifications whereas Fatheringham et al., emphasized the issue of alternatives to either home or institutional care.

Gumz and Gubrium (1972) report on the concerns of fifty (50) parents of mentally regarded young children during a series of crisis periods. This study revealed the influence, these youngsters can have on their parents' present and future concerns. Most mothers were initially concerned about the strain of caring for the handicapped infant, the readjustment of a family's daily routine, the additional time involved in caring for the child, the possibility of neglecting other family members and the ability to maintain harmony and integration. Their second concern dealt with the infant's eventual ability to get along well with others to make and keep friends and to believe that even if one does not attain the highest levels of achievement, one may still be happy. Their third concern dealt with the child's future. Mothers reported that they believed it important that their child be accepted by others, be protected from emotional stress and be happy regardless of academic achievement or job success.

The concerns reported by the fathers tended to be different. Most of them were initially concerned about the family budget and the cost of providing help for the child. Their next area of concern had to do with the handicapped infant's eventual role as a leader. his or her ability to be a winner and to assert himself or herself outside the home. The father's third area of concern involved hopes that the child would become academically successful, would have the ability to obtain training for a good job and would be able to support himself or herself.

Davis and Mackay, (1973) compared indicators of family problems in families with normal children and handicapped children. Families with subnormal children (n=70) and families with normal children (n=28) were matched on the basis of socio-economic status, religion, family size, sex, age and ordinal position of the index child. Results of the study indicate no significant difference in factors like incidence of separation or divorce, physical health of parents, mental health of parents, alcoholism and employment of mother or father. Yet there is significant difference in factors like social outings and vacations enjoyed by the two groups. Families with handicapped children could not have the benefit of social outings and vacations as much as normal families.

A report by Marshall, Hegrenes and Goldstein (1973) offers further insight into the problems, parents face as they try to manage their handicapped child's development. They observed two groups of twenty (20) mother-child pairs, one group with retarded and one with non-retarded 3–5 years olds. The mothers of the retarded children were more demanding and commanding in their verbal exchange with their children. They described the retarded child as "limited mentally and socially, thus requiring greater external" control by the parent.

McAllister et al., (1973) aimed to compare patterns of social interaction in families with behaviourally retarded child and families of a normal child. Two hundred and eighty one parents of children who are behaviourally retarded (using Vineland Scale Scores) and 784 parents of normal children constituted the sample. Frequency of intra-family patterns and extra-family patterns were studied. Less interaction within families with behaviourally retarded child was observed. There was no effect on formal community organization and affiliations on both the groups. Visits of people outside family were less frequent with behaviourally retarded child.

Richards and McIntosh (1973) commented that families with mentally handicapped children face increased financial burdens. At the same time family income may be reduced because care giving responsibilities make it difficult for the parents to work outside the home.

Holroyd (1974) and McAndrew (1976) also expressed that these families experience additional financial burdens.

Bradshaw and Lawton (1978) reported that the behaviour problems associated with mental retardation impose extra care taking demands and burden parents.

Miller and Keirn (1978) study compared MMPI (Minnesota Multiphase Personality Inventory) profiles of parents of emotionally disturbed with mentally retarded and non-clinic children. Fifty (50) mothers and fathers from each group of mentally retarded, emotionally disturbed and normal children were chosen as the sample. Parental adjustment using MMPI scores was assessed. Mothers of mentally retarded and emotionally disturbed had elevated scores. Mothers of emotionally disturbed children mostly differed from mothers of the normal children. Fathers did not significantly differ in any group.

The following are two Indian studies that dealt with problems faced by parents in raising a mentally handicapped child.

Narayan (1978) studied the impact of mentally retarded children on their families. The study explored the nature and type of problems experienced by the parents and siblings of mentally retarded children in their day-to-day living. Forty Four (44) consecutively registered cases (38 boys and 6 girls) of mental retardates aged 6–10 years with tested I.Q., below sixty seven (67) were taken. A comparable control group of forty four (44) normal kids was also taken. The tools used were an interview schedule based on that of Tizard and Grad (1961) and a modified form of Leeds Anxiety and Depression Scale to mothers.

The results showed that mental retardates coming from rural and non-nuclear families posed much less problems to their mothers. Mothers of mentally retarded kids were more prone to anxiety and depression. The presence of a retarded child often, but not always hindered the social and routine activities of the family. The mentally retarded child invariably showed severe health problems as well as temperamental problems.

Seth (1979) conducted a comparative study of maternal attitudes of retarded children and normal children. The experimental design comprised of two groups of mothers namely experimental and the control group. The experimental group comprised of thirty (30) mothers of mentally retarded children drawn from Mental Retardation Clinic and the control group consisted of thirty (30) mothers of normal children who had not sought any psychiatric help. Teachers assessment as well as psychological test results were taken into consideration for the selection of normal children.

The data was collected through case history call outs, interview schedules, psychological tests and Parental Attitude Scale.

The findings of the study clearly revealed that mothers of mentally retarded children evinced more severe and pathological attitudes than mothers of normal children.

A quantitative analysis of the interview data revealed various problems and psycho-social stresses faced by the parents in rearing their retarded children. Interview results showed that 87 per cent of the children had to be assisted in domestic behaviour as feeding. bathing, dressing and toileting, 77 per cent presented varied behaviour, disobedience, spitting, truancy, bed wetting etc. As high as 70 per cent of speech defects as mutism, defective articulation and stuttering were observed. Sixty seven per cent of children could not cope with school teaching. Fifty three per cent of miscellaneous problems include drooling of saliva, motor incoordination and inability to recognize and avoid common hazards of life.

Eighty seven per cent of mothers reported inability to carry out household work because much of their time was spent in looking after the retarded child. Eighty three per cent reported that their social life was hampered due to loss of prestige, feeling of shame, social stigma and difficulty in visiting others and entertaining guests. Eighty per cent of mothers harboured guilt feelings and attributed the child's condition to their own sins. Seventy three per cent had problems of inter personal relationship as misunderstanding and bickering among family members and marital disharmony. Sixty seven per cent indicated negative effects of mentally retarded children on other siblings.

The problem of disciplining the child was found in sixty three per cent. Forty seven per cent of mothers reported effects on the economic aspects of the family due to their retarded children.

Crnic et al., (1980) opined that the birth and continuing care of mentally retarded children are often stressful experiences for family members as these children's difficulties inevitably touch the lives of those around them.

Crnic et al., (1983) remark that as the families are affected by the presence of handicapped children, so are the children affected by their families' responses.

Beckman and Bell (1981) report that serious behaviour problems contribute to parental stress and rejection. Such problems as aggressive behaviour, stereotypic behaviour patterns and temper tantrums are great sources of stress to parents. The authors further conclude that since the parents attempt to handle these problems and as they take the child to public places they experience greater stress.

Singh and Dager (1982) analysed the records of three hundred and thirty two (332) children with primary behaviour problems to determined SES correlates of scholastic problems, speech and conduct disorders, delinquent behaviour and neurotic and psychotic reactions. The results revealed that family structure, parental education, economic status and employment of mother among others, influence behaviour. It has been argued that parents of low SES tend to seek solutions to their children's emotional problems in terms of somatic disturbance and are not conscious of their emotional and mental development as compared with parents of high SES.

Gordon et al., (1982) conducted a computer search of the records of one hundred and fourteen (114) retarded children and adolescents to determine the prevalence of behavioural and emotional problems revealing that 25 per cent of the subjects showing much problems, prevalence was also related to the degree of retardation and age.

Koller et al., (1983) examined the frequency and severity of different types of behaviour disturbances as they relate to the degree of retardation and sex. Hyperactive behaviour was most frequent among children with lower I.Q.s. Aggressive conduct disorders in childhood was most frequent among females and anti-social behaviour was more frequent among males.

Seshadri et al., (1983) studied the impact of mentally handicapped child on the family. The sample consisted of thirty (30) consecutive cases of mentally retarded children referred to psychiatry department, P.G.I., Chandigarh, together with their mothers. Children were tested for intelligence on any two of the following intelligence tests depending upon the suitability; (i) Gessell's drawing test, (ii) Seguin from board (Verma et al., 1979), (iii) Malin's Intelligence Scale for Indian children (Malin, 1969), (iv) Vineland Social Maturity Scale (Malin, undated).

The mothers were administered the following tools; (i) Parental Attitude Scale (Bhatti and Narayan, 1980), (ii) Social Burden Scale (Pai and Kapur, 1981), (iii) Marital Adjustment questionnaire (Bhat and Gauba, 1978).

This study showed that there is no significant marital disharmony. The reported burden varies from being moderately felt to severely felt. Most mothers report a favourable attitude towards the child. Significantly, the higher the level of education the more favourable is the attitude. It is also seen that the greater the degree of retardation in the child the greater is the felt burden. Child's degree of retardation is not seen to be correlated with the attitude or marital adjustment. Attitude is not significantly correlated to marital adjustment and the burden felt on the family. In view of these findings the authors suggested imparting information about mental retardation and skills training to parents which may foster favourable attitude towards their retarded children and lessen the burden felt.

Dutta (1985) in a study on adjustment problems among fifty one (51) mentally retarded boys attending regular and special schools in comparison with control group of normal boys revealed that the higher degree of neuroticism among the retarded indicated a higher level of social isolation, rejection, labelling and stigma and family stress which increased with failures and repeated frustrations.

Veena (1985) conducted a study to find out the management problems and practices of home makers with a disabled member in the family. The population of the study comprised of the families of disabled persons in the city of Vadodara. A pilot study of fifty (50) families was made to assess the extent of disability of the disabled in order to select the sample. On the basis of the results of the pilot study a purposive quota sample of twenty five (25) families was chosen keeping in mind the age and extent of disability of disabled member. The sample consisted of five families from each of the groups; orthopaedically handicapped, blind, deaf-mute, mentally retarded and cerebral palsy groups.

Data were collected by personal interview and observation of the selected households and case studies were developed. The research tools used were "extent of disability" scoring sheet, problems and practices rating scale, an attitude scale and an interview schedule.

The results indicated that the nature and extent of disability of the disabled member affected the problems faced by the family and the family had to make more efforts to solve the problems as the extent of handicap increased.

The main problem which worried most of the homemakers was care and attention of the disabled in future and anxiety about their employment and marriage. Lack of understanding about care, nature and cause of disability made them experience embarrassment at having a disability made them experience embarrassment at having a disabled family member.

The social contracts of the homemaker were restricted due to the constraints imposed by the dependence of the disabled member. On the whole the extent of problems faced in various areas increased with young children, single families and low income families. Financial problems were experienced by all but more so by the low income families.

A positive attitude on the part of the homemaker towards the disability significantly reduced the extent of problems experienced by them.

Dupont (1986) conducted a study on socio-psychiatric aspects of the young severely mentally retarded and the family. Based upon an epidemiological study (Bernsen, 1976) of severe mental retardation (in the country of Aarhus, Denmark). Dupont's first study was conducted in 1977 on thirty nine families with a child between 6 and 14 years and another study in 1980. All children were living at home and attending day institutions (with one exception). In 1984 a follow-up study was conducted with visits to all families. The computer files from 1977 are still available and data from the first survey could be compared with data produced in 1984. A schedule with the same questions as in 1977 concerning the time spent by the care taking parent(s) was worked out for each minute and produced for a week by each family.

As a basis for a questionnaire the same lists of disabilities were used; mentally retarded with delayed motor development, feeding problems, not toilet trained, passive, hyperactive, cannot be brought by public transport, hard of hearing, visually handicapped, epileptic, cerebral palsy, skin disease, weight problems, special teeth problems, special problems with supervision, financial problems and problems with siblings. For each group of problems the need for technical aid(s) and or materials and the need for care-taking personnel and time was listed.

According to the lists, a weighing of 1–3 for disabilities and variables concerning burden was given to each of the youngsters. The youngsters were grouped according to degree of burden in groups 1–4. The rating was computed using the same handicap, behaviour and Skills Schedule (HBS) as used by Bernsen (1981) and described by Wing and Could (1978).

The results of the comparative study indicated that when the child's handicap was severe and complicated the impact on the daily life of the family was also very severe.

In 1977 the families' main complaints concerned the need for supervision in many cases all day and night. The same situation was found with many cases even in 1984. However, for severely handicapped youngsters it was found that this group needed more supervision in 1984 than they did earlier. According to parents this change is due to the increase in the children's physical strength without better social adaptation, which meant that the youngsters were able to open doors or windows or evade security arrangements, but the supervision burden in these cases was less severe.

Vicki et al., (1989) examined the problematic situations experienced by mothers of mentally retarded children and those characteristics of retarded children that may influence family life problems. Thirty mothers with mentally retarded children and thirty mothers with non-retarded children constituted the sample.

Home interviews and follow up telephone interviews were conducted on seven separate evenings. During home interviews, mothers filled two measures describing their own psychological well-being, the Beck Depression Inventory (Beck, Ward, Mendelson, Mock and Erbangh, 1961) and the self-esteem sub-scale of the Jackson Personality Inventory (Jackson, 1977).

Mothers also rated the characteristics of their children using several behavioural domains taken from the adaptive Behaviour Scale (ABS Lambert, Windmiller, Tharinger and Cole, 1975). Specifically two scores were derived (a) a measure of the child's level of Independent Functioning (e.g., initiation, cooperation and consideration) and (b) a measure of the extent of Problem Behaviour exhibited by the child (e.g., aggression, hyperactive tendencies and emotional instabilities).

Finally mothers with retarded children were interviewed about family life problems, using both open ended and structured questions of particular interest were problematic situations or events that were related to the retarded children's influence on family life. Here the interviewers provided these mothers with a brief description of seven family life problem areas that may stem from rearing a retarded child.

1. Limited time available to care givers
2. Child management difficulties
3. Concern regarding the disabled child's well-being
4. Financial burdens
5. Dysfunctional family interaction patterns
6. Inadequacies in the support received from friends and relations.
7. Negative involvement with community services and professionals.

Questions focuses on mother's perceptions of how the target child's retardation gave rise to problems in each area.

Multivariate analysis revealed significant group differences in both child characteristics and in duration of maternal involvement in child-oriented activities. No overall group differences in maternal well-being emerged. Child welfare issues and restrictive time demands were the most intense family problems reported by mothers with retarded children. Ratings of more intense family problems were associated with more time spent with the child and more symptoms of maternal depression.

Peshawaria et al., (1988) reported that one of the most sought after area of service by parents of mentally handicapped children is the management of behaviour problems. Peshawaria et al., (1990) conducted a study with three hundred (300) cases of mentally handicapped persons with reported behaviour problems registered at National Institute for Mentally Handicapped (NIMH). The parental needs with regard to behaviour problems in their mentally handicapped children were analysed in the following twelve areas;

1. Physical harm towards others
2. Damages property
3. Misbehaves with others
4. Temper tantrums
5. Wanders
6. Disobedience
7. Repetitive behaviours
8. Self injurious behaviour
9. Restless, physically overactive
10. Odd behaviour
11. Fears
12. Sexual problems

The trends in parental needs of behaviour problems were analysed in terms of severity, sex and age of the mentally handicapped persons, type of family and area of residence. The results indicated that parents predominantly seek help for managing problems of disobedience (15.8%) in their mentally handicapped children, and the least perceived behaviour problem is in the sexual area (0.9%). This could be more due to inhibitions in the parents to openly report on such matters at first contact.

In terms of severity of mental handicap the trends appear to be similar for the mild and moderate groups where "disobedience" and "physical harm towards others" are perceived as major behaviour problems. "Odd behaviours" are perceived more common with severe and profound groups. With regard to age behaviour problems decrease with increasing age. "Wandering" is more common with male handicapped children than with females, whereas "temper tantrums" and "fears" are more common with females than with males.

In terms of family variable both parents from nuclear as well as non-nuclear families perceive "disobedience" as the major behaviour problem in their mentally handicapped children.

With regard to area of residence parents from urban set-up report more behaviour problems related to "disobedience" (17.1%)

whereas parents from rural set up report greater frequency of "physical harm towards others".

Peshawaria et al., (1990) conducted another survey on teacher's perceptions of problem behaviours among mentally handicapped persons in special school settings. The survey covers two hundred and eighty eight (288) institutions working for the mentally handicapped in India. A problem behaviour check-list comprising of a broad range of twelve (12) categories was developed and mailed to these institutions out of which five hundred and thirty (530) teachers from one hundred and forty eight (148) institutions responded. A test re-test reliability co-efficient was attempted by remaining the problem 'Behaviour Checklist' to a select group of one hundred and twenty seven (127) teachers from eighteen (18) schools for the mentally handicapped after a lapse of eight weeks. Reliability correlation coefficient was found to be 0.68.

The main results of the survey indicate that problem behaviours predominantly in the form of "restless and physically overactive" "inattentive behaviours" and "misbehaves with others" respectively. Teacher's experience appears to be an important index in the perception of number of behaviour problems in mentally handicapped persons. Especially teachers with more than five years of experience perceive significantly greater number of behaviour problems than their lesser experienced colleagues.

Purnima (1990) remarked that the parents of developmentally delayed children are hit the hardest, and they must muster internal and external resources to met the special needs of the child; as well as to handle their own reactions. She further concluded that the problems experienced by parents of such children vary at different stages of the life cycle and thus intervention strategies will also differ.

Thressiakurtty and Narayan (1990) conducted a study on parental perceptions of problems and expectations regarding their mentally retarded children. This study included parents of one hundred adolescent and adult mentally retarded persons registered during the year 1985–86 in the NIMH general service. An analysis has been made on complaints and expectations perceived and expressed by the parents with regard to their children. Result indicate that inappropriate social behaviours rank highest (86) with regard to complaints followed by poor abilities (48) which is the next important component for social competence with regard to parental expectations. The study also revealed that the number of expectations of the parents from their retarded children is relatively less when compared to the number of complaints. The expectations of the parents are not in relation to the complaints. Most of the parents expect vocational training for their child while majority of the parents complain of social incompetence which hinders successful vocational training and job placement.

The investigators felt that it is necessary that the parents are informed clearly about their child's level of functioning and capabilities so that their expectations can be realistic.

Ramgopal and Rao (1994) attempted to assess the behaviour disorders in moderately mentally retarded and their relation to parental attitude. The study was conducted at three special schools for mentally retarded and their relation to parental attitude. The study was conducted at three special schools for mentally retarded children at Bangalore. The sample comprised of parents (either father or mother) of sixty (60) moderately mentally retarded children of both sexes in the age range of 8–12 years. Conner's Parent Rating Scale was administered to assess the learning and conduct problems which were present to a high degree and psychosomatic disturbances, impulsive hyperactive and anxiety problems to a low degree. The findings on the parental attitude scale showed negative attitude of the parents towards the moderately mentally retarded children. There was a non-significant negative correlation between behaviour disorder and parental attitude of the moderately mentally retarded children.

Studies Related to Family Stress with a Mentally Handicapped Child

Hill (1949) popularly known as the father of family stress theory published a model which is the organizing framework for an examination of critical issues outstanding in the area of families under stress. He suggested that the family's definition of an event is seen as a threat to that status, goals and objectives of the family—is an important determinant of crisis severity.

Hill (1958) after studying a number of father absent families during World War II formulated his ABC–X model of family stress theory which provided a substantial base for the scientific inquiry of family stress.

His framework for family stress theory focused on three variables :

A — the provoking event or stressor.

B — the family's resources or strengths at the time of the event.

C — the meaning attached to the event by the family (individually and collectively).

X — Outcome : the resulting degree of stress (high strained, low-managed) or crisis.

Numerous studies of the families raising children with mental handicap have emphasized the stress, crisis, chronic sorrow and strain present in these families. Menolascino and Wolfensberger (167) mentioned three types of crisis patterns in; families with a mentally retarded child.

a) the novelty shock crisis or the shock of initial diagnosis;

b) the crisis of personal values characterized by a reaction of anguish and chronic sorrow stemming from the destruction of their over determined expectations of the child; and

c) the reality crisis stemming from external forces related to difficulties of raising the child such as physical demands and social pressures.

Family stress is defined by McCubbin and Patterson (1983) as a state that arises from an actual or perceived demand and capability imbalance in the family's functioning, which is characterized by a multi-dimensional demand for adjustment or adaptive behaviour. Stress is, therefore, not stereotypic but rather varies depending upon the nature of the situation, the characteristics of the family unit and the psychological or physical well-being of its members. Stress becomes distress when it is subjectively defined as unpleasant or undesirable by the family unit.

Boss (1988) described family stress as pressure on the family. It is a disturbance of the family's steady state, i.e., the family system is upset, pressured and disturbed and not at rest. Family stress therefore, is a change in the family's equilibrium. The author further explained that the family stress need not always be bad and it becomes problematic only when the degree of stress in the family system reaches a level at which family members become dissatisfied or show symptoms of disturbance.

Family stress may result in (a) lowered performance in the family's usual routines and tasks, (b) the occurrence of physical or emotional symptoms in individual family members. These symptoms signal danger when the level of stress on a family's structure increases.

While trying to understand family stress it is necessary to keep in mind that family stress does not have to end in trouble. In highly stressed but functional families there is flexibility in family rules, roles and problem solving skills. The family members must be able to change constantly to adapt to the situation at hand and there must be a continuous negotiation between family's pressures and supports. Such flexible family systems can withstand a lot of pressure.

Parenting itself can be generally a stressful life event, (Giband, Wallston and Wandersman, 1978) and the manifestation of major and child problems may be the most significant of stress across a range of unpleasant parental effects (Weinberg and Richardson, 1981). Mothers of children exhibiting hyperactivity, conduct disorders and other types of handicapping conditions such as cerebral palsy and developmental delay, participate in transactions with their children that are more stressful, or less rewarding and provide considerably less positive feed back than in the case for mothers of normal children (Barkley, 1981; Patterson, 1976, 1980; Kogan, Tyler and Turner, 1974; Long and Moore, 1979 and Kogan, 1980).

Many of the behaviours commonly exhibited by problem children are perceived by parents as annoying, noxious and stressful (Jones, Reid and Patterson (1975). The following are some of the studies on family stress with a handicapped child.

Jain (1967) examined the social problems related to the

presence of a mentally retarded child in the family using a sample of twenty eight (28) normal children and twenty eight (28) mentally retarded children. Findings indicated that parental feelings were marked by anxiety about the future. Constant psychological stress, negative effect on the other siblings, misunderstandings within the family, decreased interaction with the neighbours and relatives and economic loss were significant factors associated with the families of retarded children.

Cummings (1976) compared the psychological adjustment of fathers of mentally retarded with chronically ill and healthy children. The sample consisted of 60 natural fathers of each category of children from intact families. All the families in the study had more than one child. Target children's age ranged from 4–13 years. Standard measures included were Sentence Completion Test, Self Acceptance Scale of Berger Inventory, Shoben's Parental Attitudes Inventory, and Edwards Personal Preference Schedule.

The results indicated that the fathers of mentally retarded had more depressive feeling and more pre-occupation with the child. They exhibited more inferiority as fathers and had general lack of relationship gratification with low enjoyment of the child. The fathers had greater negative impact from fathering than those of chronically ill children.

Beckman's (1983) focus of study was to examine the relationship between child characteristics and stress reported by mothers. The child characteristics considered were rate of development, social responsiveness, temperament, repetitive, stereotypic behaviours and additional care giving demands. The sample consisted of 31 infants and mothers. The age range of the infants was 6.6–36.6 months. The tools used were questionnaire on resources and stress (Holroyd, 1974) Holmes and Rehe (1967) Schedule of Recent experience.

The results of Beckman indicated that four of the child characteristics, temperament, responsiveness repetitive behavioural patterns and care-giving demands, were significantly related to the amount of stress reported by the mothers on QRS, but not significantly related to the amount of stress reported on the schedule of recent experience.

Single parents experienced more stress but there is no significant difference between amount of stress reported by mothers of boys and girls.

No significant difference between child's age and stress was reported.

Crnic et al., (1983) reviewed the research concerning families with mentally retarded children and commented that the results are inconsistent and sometimes yielded contradictory results. They further stated that this inconsistency is partly due to methodological inadequacies and a narrow focus on unidimensional variables with unimodel measurements.

The authors finally proposed a model to understand the adaptation of families with mentally retarded children focusing on 'stress' 'coping' and 'family ecology'. The model integrates concepts from the distinct bodies of research namely stress, coping and ecological influences on development and functioning. The presence of the retarded child represents a significant on-going stressor within the family, precipitating numerous minor and major crises. Subsequent familial response to each stress will involve the various coping resources available both to the individual and the family as a whole. The coping resources available as well as how and when they are used are mediated by the various ecological domains in which the family members interact. So in this model the authors attempted to explain the range of familial adaptation as a response to stress moderated by the interaction of available coping resources and ecological contexts.

Friedrich et al., (1983) conducted two studies, one to develop a shorter and psycho metrically stronger inventory, later called as Questionnaire on Resources and Stress (QRS-F) and another study was a report on an independent validation of this short form.

A total of 289 QRSs were completed by parents and collected during a number of research studies involving parental coping and adaptation (Friedrich, 1979; Friedrich and Friedrich, 1981) in families of handicapped children. The QRS was mailed to parents involved in the studies and this was completed by the biological mother in 71 per cent of the cases, the biological father in 20 per cent of the cases and an adoptive or step parent in the remaining 9 per cent. Mean educational level for the parents was 12.4 years for the mothers, and 12.7 years for the fathers.

Of the 289 children 12 per cent had no handicapping condition, 10 per cent had motoric disabilities but no associated mental retardation, 28 per cent were deaf, blind but were neither motorically nor mentally retarded (I.Q. $>$ 80) and 50 per cent were mentally retarded (I.Q. $\leq$ 70). Of those children with mental retardation 38 per cent were also diagnosed as having cerebral palsy. The children ranged in age from 22 months to 18 years (mean 9.5 years) and were nearly equally divided by sex (51 per cent male, 49 per cent female). Vast majority of these children were Caucasian and 90 per cent living at home.

The investigation involved an item analysis of the 285 items QRS (which reduced the length of the QRS to 52 items, forming QRS-F). The initial factor analysis of these 52 items with a heterogeneous groups of parents of handicapped and non-handicapped children and determined the validity of these factors with an independent sample.

Four orthogonal (independent) factors emerged suggestion that the QRS-F is an instrument measuring the broad categories of parent and family problems, pessimism, child characteristics and physical incapacitation in those families with a handicapped child.

In the second validation study 40 mothers of children who were then attending self-contained special education classes in a school district in the metropolitan Seatle area constituted the sample. The children ranged in age from 5 to 18 years (mean 12.2) and all of them had been identified as atleast mentally retarded (I.Q. $<$ 70).

The mothers were given the QRS-F along with the Beck Depression Inventory, Marlowe-Crowne Social Desirability Scale and a checklist of disturbing behaviour problems of children.

A correlation matrix was generated with the four, QRS-F factors-the Beck Depression Inventory, the Marlowe Crowne and the problem checklist. Significant correlation between the independent measures and these four QRS-F factors would serve to indicate the nature of what each of these factors are measuring. The results suggested that the problems faced by these families are clearly multidimensional and that the score on a given dimension cannot predict or be predicted from knowledge of the scores of the remaining directions.

Mash and Johnston (1983) studied the parental perceptions of child behaviour, parenting self-esteem and mothers reported stress of younger and older hyperactive and normal children. Forty (40) families with a hyperactive child and fifty one (51) families with normal children participated in the study. Hyperactivity rating scale (Conner, 1972) Child Behaviour Checklist (CBCL, Achenbach, 1978; Achenback and Edelbrock, 1981), Parenting sense of Competence Scale (PSOC, Giband, Wallston and Wandersman), and Parenting Stress Index (PSI, Abidin and Burke, 1978 were the instruments used for the collection of data.

Results indicated that the parenting self-esteem was lower in parents of hyperactive than in parents of normal children. Self-esteem related to skill/knowledge as a parent was age related, with parents of older hyperactives reporting the lowest levels whereas self-esteem related to valuing/comfort in the parenting role was not related to the child's age. Mothers of hyperactives especially younger hyperactives reported markedly higher levels of stress associated with both child characteristics such as distractibility and degree of bother and with their own feelings such as depression, self-blame and social isolation.

Consistent inverse relationships were found between parental self-esteem and perceptions of child problems, whereas ratings of child disturbance and maternal stress were positively correlated. Moudgil et al., (1985) had undertaken an investigation to understand the quantum of stress on the parents of mentally retarded children. Three aspects, namely, what social and emotional support systems they adopt to cope with the stress. How the interpersonal relations of the parents are affected and how the social image of the family is affected in the community because of the retarded child were studied. A Semi structure Interview Schedule (prepared to tap information regarding various stresses and problems of these unfortunate children) and the Measure of Emotional Support was administered to the eighteen (18) pairs of parents of mentally retarded children.

It is found that because of the mentally retarded child in the family, parents feel depressed most of the time, worry about getting their children admitted to school, have to pay more attention to retarded child, and their marital harmony and relations with their family members are disturbed. The social image of the parents is also affected. It was found that those parents who get maximum social and emotional support from spouse, family members, parents, relatives and friends experience less stresses and problems as compared to those parents who are not getting much social and emotional support. It was also found that the parents could not achieve some of their life goals and when the child was female it created more social and emotional problems.

Wikler (1986) made an exploratory study on the periodic stresses of families of older mentally retarded children. The relationship of transitions and stress in 60 families of older mentally retarded children were examined. Families whose offspring were entering adolescence (11–15 years old) and young adulthood (20–21 years old) were identified as being in transition. They were contrasted with families whose offsprings were not of those ages. Families were assessed once and then again after two years. The results indicated no significant differences between the transition and non-transition families on Schedules of Recent Events Scores for their time period. In contrast the family stress scores on the questionnaire on Resources and stress were significantly higher at both times for transition families than for non-transition families. This study has identified two specific periods of transition of older retarded children which are associated with increased disruption for families.

Wilton and Renaut (1986) examined the family stress levels using the Questionnaire on Resources and Stress (QRS) in 42 New Zealand families with pre-school intellectually handicapped (moderately and severely retarded) children and 42 families with non-handicapped pre-school children. Maternal age was employed as a blocking factor (less than 30 years versus 30 years and above). The families with intellectually handicapped children showed significantly higher stress levels on 13 of the 15 QRS scales, but maternal age did not appear to be implicated in family stress levels.

The results suggested that stress levels are somewhat elevated in families with pre-school children, the tendency being particularly marked in families with intellectually handicapped children. The implications of these findings for family intervention and support programmes are considered, together with the need for research into the various ecological contexts of the individual, family, peer group and social institutions.

Donovan (1988) investigated the mothers perceptions of family stress and ways of coping whit adolescents who were autistic or had mental retardation. Sample comprised of thirty six (36) mothers from each group. Stress was measured with QRS Revised from (Friedrich, Greenberg and Crinc, 1983). The Locke Wallace Marital Adjustment Scale Short Form (Locke and Wallace, 1959) was used as the measure of marital adjustment and an indirect measure of the extent to which child stress impacted on broader family functioning. The Coping Health Inventory for parents Form D (McCubbin and Cauble, 1979) was used as the measure of parental coping.

Results indicated group differences among maternal reports of family stress. All comparisons of child related stress revealed that mothers with an adolescents who was autistic perceived greater level of family stress than did mothers with an adolescent who had mental retardation. Marital adjustment did not differ by group. Further, maternal coping styles were consistent across groups, indicating that mothers with adolescents who had a handicap relied heavily on community resources and professional help for coping.

The findings suggested that when the demands associated with parenting adolescent with handicaps exceed the resources of the family, mothers choose to cope by actively seeking support, advice and help outside the family system.

Minnes (1988) studied the family resources and stress associated with having a mentally retarded child. Basing on the concepts drawn from family stress theory and current empirical information on families of handicapped children, the investigator analyzed the factors influencing parental adjustment to stress associated with such children living at home.

Parental stress was measured with QRS-Short-Form (Holroyd, 1982), Family Environment Scale (Moos and Moos, 1981) was used to measure internal family resources, Family Crisis–Orientation Personal Evaluation Scale (McCubbin and Thompson, 1987) was used to measure external family resources and child and parent characteristics were noted with a checklist. Sixty (60) mothers filled up the above four questionnaires.

Results of multiple regression analysis indicated that child characteristics and the family's crisis meeting resources were significant predictors of various forms of stress. Child characteristics and family crisis meeting resources did not emerge together as significant predictors of stress in all regression analysis and when they did emerge significant together the proportion of variance accounted for was not consistent in each case. The varying percentages of variance accounted for by individual predictors in this study highlight the complexity of the processes involved in stress management and coping.

Singer et al., (1988) evaluated the efficacy of self-management treatment package for reducing the psychological distress of parents of children with severe handicaps. Thirty six (36) parents of school aged children with severe handicaps were randomly assigned to a treatment group and a waiting list as control group.

Three kinds of measure were used—descriptive, dependent and social validation. The behavioural Development Survey was used to measure children's levels of adaptive and aberrant behaviours and social support was measured using the Inventory of Parents' Experiences (Crnic, Ragozin, Greenberg and Robinson, 1981). A fifty four (54) item self report survey that measures parents' contacts with formal and informal sources of social support and their satisfaction with them was also conducted. Stress associated with parenting a child with handicaps was measured with QRS-short from (Friedrich et al., 1983).

The two dependent variables–parental anxiety and depression were measured State Trait Anxiety Inventory (Spielberger, Gorsuch and Lushene, 1970) and Beck Depression Inventory (Beck, Ward, Mendelson, Mock and Erbaugh, 1961). A social validation measure was used to assess parents' satisfaction with the treatment procedures and their evaluation of the success of the various treatment components (Kazdin and Matson, 1981).

The parents in the treatment group were taught techniques of (a) self monitoring stressful events and physiological reactions to them, (b) muscle relaxation skills and (c) modification of cognitions associated with distress. The treatment group and the control group significantly differed in the mean score on the behaviour Development Survey. The mean score of the treatment group was much lower than the control group indicating increased parental depression.

Results suggested that stress management training can be added in the pool of interventions that have been found to be helpful to parents of children with handicaps.

Flynt and Wood (1989) examined the perceptions of family stress and coping behaviour of ninety (90) mothers with the moderately mentally retarded child. Telephone interviews were used to collect the data from three groups of mothers (30 in each group) depending on the child's chronological age. The targeted ages were school entry (ages 6 to 9), early adolescence (ages 12 to 15) and young adults (ages 18 to 21). The age range of the mothers was from 22 to 60 years.

Instruments used were QRS Short Form (Friedrich et al., 1983) and Coping Health Inventory especially prepared for the study. Preliminary analysis for evaluating efficacies of specified two-way interactions (Race X Marital status, Race SES and SES X Marital Status) showed no significant differences in effects of either interaction on maternal perception of family stress or coping behaviour. But the multivariate analysis of variance yielded significant main effects from stress and coping scores and maternal age, race, SES and marital status. Child's age did not significantly affect the stress and coping scores. Black mothers reported lower perceived family stress than did white mothers and reported higher scores on coping. Health Inventory indicating greater utilization of coping strategies centered around intra-family resources and social support. Older mothers reported lower perceived family stress than did young mothers. Although the investigators identified patterns of coping behaviour exhibited by these mothers, further research of the formal and informal support systems utilized by mothers with a moderately mentally retarded child could provide helpful information.

Frey et al., (1989) examined the mediating influences of child characteristics, social network, parent beliefs and coping styles on parenting stress, family adjustment and psychological distress of mothers and fathers. Subjects were forty eight (48) mothers and forty eight (48) fathers of young children with handicaps. The age of the handicapped children ranged from 32 mothers to 168 months. Instruments for data collection include : Daily Parenting Hassles (Crnic and Greenberg, 1984) QRS-F (Friedrich, Greenberg and Crnic, 1983), the Family Relationships Inventory (Moos, Insel and Humphrey, 1974), Marital Adjustment Scale (Locke and Wallace, 1959), the Family Support Scale (Dunst, Jenkins and Trivette, 1984), the Brief Symptom Inventory (Derogatis, 1975), Coping Checklist (Vitaliano et al,) and Comparative Appraisals Scale designed for the study. Interview measures were Vineland Adaptive Behaviour Scale (Sparrow, Balla and Cicchetti, 1985) and Home Quality Rating Scale (Meyers, Mink and Nihira 1981).

Results indicated that child characteristics predicted mother's and father's parenting stress and father's psychological distress. Parental beliefs systems predicted all three parent outcomes for mothers and fathers. Coping styles predicted psychological distress and father's family adjustment. Social network predicted family adjustment and father's psychological distress. Psychological distress was low in mothers who had either a positive belief system or a non-critical family network. Findings support the value of a multidimensional examination of family characteristics that mediate the impact of a child's handicap.

Crnic and Greenberg (1990) explored the minor parenting stresses among seventy four (74) mother child pairs participating in a longitudinal project. At the time of the study the children's age was five (5) years. Parenting Daily Hassles (PDH), Satisfaction with Parenting Scale (SWPS), Family Environment Scale (FES, Moos and Moos, 1981), General Life Satisfaction (GLS), Life Experiences Survey (LES, Sarason et al., 1978), Behaviour Symptom Index (BSI, Derogatis and Spencer, 1982), Child Behaviour Checklist (Achenback and Edelbrock, 1983) were the instruments used for collection of necessary data.

Analysis indicated that life stress and parenting daily hassles significantly predicted aspects of child, parent and family status. Hassles, however, proved to be a more powerful stress construct. Further analysis indicated that mother's social support moderated the influence of hassles on indices of maternal behaviour.

Leyser and Dekel (1990) studied eighty two (82) Israeli families residing in a religious section of Jerusalem. Each family had atleast one child with a moderate to severe disability attending a special education school.

Data were collected through structured interviews on 34 items eliciting information about background, impact of one disabled member on family life and siblings, areas of stress and availability of personal and professional support systems.

A step-wise multiple regression was computed to identify critical variables that may help to explain the degree to which the family felt stressed. Thirty eight per cent of the parents felt that the disability affected the family "much" or "very much". Seventeen per cent responded that there was "some" effect and 45 per cent indicated that the child's disability had very little or no effect.

Results indicated that in cases where parents experienced more daily pressures (i.e., financial constraints, lack of services, lack of time and feelings of stigma) the disabled child was a boy, the mother was older and the number of children in the family was smaller. They reported being more stressed by the child's disability. About 50 per cent were rated by a school professional as coping and adjusting effectively. Many mothers and fathers maintained close contact with their own parents, frequently discussed the child's problems and sought advice from health care professional and from their spiritual leaders. Most families needed financial assistance.

Findings seem to be consistent with those reported by other investigators and show that many of the families with a disabled member experienced increased levels of stress and greater family problems.

Beckman (1991) compared mother's and father's perception of the effect of young children with and without disabilities. Subjects were 54 mothers and 54 fathers of children. Half of the children had handicaps and half did not have any handicap. All the children were from intact families. Groups were matched with respect to the child's sex and age (ranged from 18-72 months). Children with disabilities were all moderately to severely delayed but were heterogeneous with respect to type of disability–10 had cerebal palsy, 2 autism, 5 multiple disabilities, 3 genetic disorders resulting in developmental delay and 7 general delays of unknown origin.

Parenting Stress Index (Abidin, 1983) was used as the measure of stress. Carolina Parent Support Scale (Bristol, 1979) was used as the measure of social support, which was adapted from a scale used by Bronfenbrenner et al., (1977). Interview method was adopted using these two instruments for collection of information.

Each parent was also asked to complete care giving questionnaire designed to tap the number of additional or unusual care giving needs presented by the child in the areas of feeding, handling or medical care. Parents indicated the presence or absence of each of the difficulties identified on the scale and items were summed to yield a total care-giving score.

Results indicated significant differences between mothers and fathers on parent domain of the Parent Stress Index. Mothers reported more stress than did fathers, however, the direction of difference depended on the individual scale. Parents of children with disabilities reported more care-giving requirements and stress in all domains. Stress was negatively associated with informal support for bother parents and positively associated with increased care giving requirements for mothers.

Bromley and Blacher (1991) studied sixty three (63) parents of children with severe handicaps who were recently placed out of home and were interviewed regarding their reasons for placement. Of the sixty three (63) parents interviewed, fifty eight (58) were mothers, two (2) were grandmothers and three (3) were fathers. All were the primary care providers to the child prior to placement. Parents ranged in age from nineteen (19) to sixty eight (68) years. SES was measured utilizing Duncan (1961) scale.

Results indicated that parent's decision to place was not based on any one strong influence; rather it was influenced by a number of factors working together. Parent's perceived daily stress, the child's low level of functioning and child's behaviour problems strongly influenced the placement decision. Lack of appropriate support services were only moderately influential in the decision. Age of the child did not influence placement decision.

Orr et al., (1991) suggested a new model of understanding stress and coping in families with children who have mental retardation. Subjects were eighty six (86) parents (80 mothers, 3 fathers, 2 grandmothers and 1 grandfather) of trainable mentally retarded children whose age ranged from 5 to 21 years. Instruments used were Parenting Stress Index (Abidin, 1986), Family Inventory of Resources and Management (McCubbin and Comean, 1987) and Family Crisis Oriented Personal Evaluation Scales (McCubbin, Olson and Larsen, 1987).

The Double ABCX model of family stress and coping was evaluated using path analysis to determine the casual ordering of variables.

The families use of resources (B) and their perception of stress or event (C) were examined to determine their relation to stress (A) and stress experiences (X). The casual ordering of the model suggested an ACBX relation rather than an ABCX relation. The results suggested the need to listen to the families and to explore their perceptions about their children, the disability and how it is affecting the family.

Baxter (1992) investigated the impact of perceptions on stress experienced by parents of children with intellectual disabilities. Sample comprised of 60 parents of 3-5 years old children, 35 parents of 10-12 years old children and 36 parents of 17-19 years teenagers.

Two interview schedules were used, one covering the basic demographic data and the other covering major stress measures.

Parental stress attributed to care and management of the child with an intellectual disability was found to be related to the extent of child's dependence and the extent of child's behaviour problems. An interesting finding of the study is the curvilinear pattern of relationship between stress and the appraised significance perceptions across the three age categories.

Most importantly, these perceptions of parents when added to dependence and behaviour problems of the child, account for 50 per cent of the variance in explaining stress in the case of parents of 10-12 years old but only 15 per cent in the cases of parents of 3-5 years old. The results of the study further support the view that parental perception are a vital component to the formulations of family focused interventions.

Rousey et al., (1992) commented that stress in families with children who have special needs, which has been the focus of much research interest is usually assessed solely from a maternal perspective. But unlike the other investigations in this study, QRS-F (Friedrich, Greenberg and Crnic, 1983) was completed separately by mothers and fathers of children with severe disabilities.

Fifty one (51) mothers and forty two (42) fathers constituted the sample. The results of the factor analysis did not reveal overwhelming differences between factors and between parent mean scores. Gender of the parent seems to have minimal effect on perceptions of stress and coping. Overall validity of the QRS-F for use with both mothers and fathers of children with severe disabilities was supported.

Krauss (1993) designed a study to determine whether there are significant differences between mothers and fathers of young children with disabilities in the amount of the child related and parenting stress. Child-related stress refers to behavioural and temperamental qualities of a child and parenting stress refers to dimensions of parent's functioning.

Subjects were one hundred and twenty one (121) mothers and fathers of toddlers with disabilities. Instruments used were Parenting Stress Index (Abidin, 1983), Child Improvements Locus of Control Scales (De Villis et al., 1985), Parent Support Scale (Dunst, Jenkins and Trivette, 1984), Family Adaptability and Cohesion Evaluation Scales II (Olson, Bell and Portuer, 1982) and Bayley Scales of Infant Development (Bayley, 1969).

The multivariate analysis of variance revealed no significant differences associated with the child's type of disability between mothers' and fathers' scores for child related or parenting stress, Locus of Control, Family functioning or size of their support networks. However, fathers reported more stress related to their child's temperament and their relationship to their child. Mothers reported more stress from the personal consequences of parenting. Fathers were more sensitive to the effects of the family environment whereas mothers were more affected by their personal support networks. These similarities and differences suggested by the findings of the study would enable the service providers to effectively, help both the parents of children with disabilities.

Kravetz et al., (1993) examined how mothers and fathers cope with tensions involved in the day-to-day struggle of raising a child with mental retardation. Further more, it was investigated whether the ways in which mothers and fathers cope with these tensions are related to the school adjustment of the child. Fifty seven (57) parent pairs with a child with mental retardation were included in the sample. The age range of the children was from 9–12 years and all the families were from a medium to low socio-economic background and were intact.

The instruments used for the study were ways of coping scale (Folkman and Lazarus, 1980) and Adaptive Behaviour Scale (ABS) (Nihira et al., 1974). Results indicated that the father's emotion focused coping was found to be positively and significantly related to their children's school achievement. Mother's problem focused coping correlated positively with their children's constructive behaviour and negatively with their children's behaviour disturbance. Although a statistically significant difference was found between mother's and father's use of coping strategies, this differences does not seem to be a consequence of the relations between mother's and father's coping strategies and particular aspects of their children's school adjustment. Fathers reported using emotion focused coping less often than did mothers even though, a statistically significant relation was discovered between fathers emotion focused coping and their children's school achievement.

Orr et al., (1993) studied stress experienced by families with a child who has development delay. Mothers with children ranging in age from 2 to 18 years were assigned to a pre-school, middle childhood group and the adolescent group. Parenting Stress Index (Abidin, 1986) was used to measure the stress. Hollingshead's (1975) Four Factors Index Social Status was used to measures social status of families. Parent's perceptions of different handicapping conditions and behaviour problems were the other variables studied.

Results indicated that children belonging to all the three groups were strong sources of stress for mothers. The second trend that is evident was that mothers in the middle childhood group reported consistently higher stress scores than did mothers in the other two groups on both parent and child Domain Scores.

The Parenting Stress Index Social Isolation sub-scale indicated no differences in the social support received by the three groups, which suggests that the observed differences were relatively independent of familial or extra familial resources available to the mother.

The middle childhood group reported a significantly greater frequency of behaviour problems than did the adolescent group.

(means 2.8 and 2.0 respectively (75) = 2,15, $P < 0.05$). The results further suggested that the behaviour problems appear to be a strong predictor of parenting stress index for both the groups.

Constant stress may be often viewed as a burden. The following studies indicated how the families felt it as a burden to raise a child with mental handicap.

Studies Related to Family Burden and Handicapped Child

Goldman as long back as 1962 considered family member whose social functioning is inadequate or affected will lead to greater family burden. The existence of burden indicate the breakdown of reciprocal arrangements that people maintain in their relationships, so that, some persons in the family have to do more than their fair share. Since they do more than what they have to do, their activities are often restricted.

The term family burden can be defined operationally as the extent of suffering experienced by the family of mentally handicapped child due to various problems encountered with regard to financial conditions, routine family interaction, leisure, physical and mental health of other members of the family caused by the handicapped family member.

Jain and Satyavathi (1969) and Kaur (1977) opined that the persence of a child with mental handicap can become a source of continuous stress and burden on family members.

Sethi and Sitholey (1986) reported parental burden in the form of interfaces in their family routine or leisure and recreation, which even resulted in social, marital familial and emotional problems in the home settings of individuals with mental handicap.

Erickson and Upshur (1989) conducted an exploratory study to see the difference between mothers of children with disabilities and without disabilities in their perceptions regarding child care-taking burden, father's participation in child care-taking and burden, father's participation in child care-taking and satisfaction with social support. The sample consisted of 202 mothers of infants with Down's syndrome, motor impairment, developmental delay and no known disabilities. All measures were self reports based on the mother's perceptions. Significant differences among the four groups were found on child care-taking, difficulty of feeding, bathing and dressing and care-taking time. Second finding was that fathers of infants with disabilities did not perform more care-taking tasks, than did fathers of infants without disabilities. Mothers of infants without disabilities were significantly less satisfied than mothers of infants with disabilities.

Sequeira et al., (1990) attempted to assess the burden perceived by mothers of the mentally handicapped children in relation to the degree of retardation and the sex of their handicapped child. The second objective of the study was to know the coping styles used by the mothers of handicapped children in the management of stress.

The sample was purposive and consisted of 55 mothers of male (N=30) and female (N=25) mentally retarded children in the age range of 5–12 years with moderate (N=30) and severe (N=25) degree of retardation seeking consultation for the first time at the mental retardation clinic NIMHANS. Pai and Kapur's (1981) schedule was used to assess the perceived burden. A coping checklist adapted from Moos (1982) consisted of coping styles.

Results indicated that there were no significant differences in the perceived burden with reference to the sex of the child. Significant differences were found by way of disruption of routine family activities when degree of retardation was taken into account. Denial, Rehearsal of outcome, finding a purpose and seeking emotional support were the commonly utilized coping styles by the mothers of the mentally handicapped children.

Tangri and Verma (1992) studied the social burden felt by mothers of the handicapped children. The sample consisted of mothers of 50 physically handicapped and 50 mentally handicapped children in the age range of 8–15 years. The I.Qs of mentally handicapped children were in the range of 35–70. Physically handicapped children suffered from orthopaedic handicap and had normal intelligence. Majority of the subjects in the sample belonged to Chandigarh and adjoining areas.

Social Burden Scale (Pai and Kapur, (1981), a semi structured interview schedule used to assess the burden placed on families. It consists of 24 items arranged in 6 different categories : (1) Financial

Burden, (2) disruption of routine family activities, (3) disruption of family leisure, (4) disruption of family interaction, (5) effect on physical health of others and (6) effect on mental health of others. Reported reliability figures ranged from 0.87 to 0.90.

A2 × 2 analysis of variance with 2 levels of handicap (physical and mental) was applied on each of the sub-scale of social burden. Results of analysis of variance for disruption in family routine, disruption in family interaction and the overall burden with the presence of handicapped child showed a significant effect of handicap. The mothers of mentally handicapped children reported, higher social burden than those of the physically handicapped children.

Comparing the burden perceived by mothers of handicapped boys and girls it was found that disruption in family leisure and effect on mental health of the mothers were reported more often by the mothers of female children. Majority of the mothers (both the handicapped groups) rated the overall burden as moderate to severe.

Venkatesan and Das (1994) attempted to explore trends in the nature and type of reported burden on family members in received/implementing home based training programme for their children with mental handicap. The mentally handicapped sample comprised of seventy (70) individuals belonging to various SES and severity levels including forty four (44) males and twenty six (26) females in the age range of 3 moths to 20 years seeking home based training at the National Institute for the Mentally Handicapped (NIMH).

A semi-structured interview schedule exclusively prepared for this purpose was used to elicit data in the form of specific verbalizations of perceived burden by family members in receiving/implementing home based training programmes for their children with mental handicap. The results indicated that the presence of a child with mental handicap can indeed become a source of perceived burden for family members even though it does not appear to be significantly influenced by specific variables like child, family characteristics or some characteristics of service delivery. Further the nature or type of perceived burden by family members may range from difficulties in transportation of child to place of service delivery, management of child's behaviour problems, disruption of their daily routine, economic, physical and or social burden. A small percentage of parents also reported "No burden" in seeking home based training programmes.

In view of the above findings transportation facilities for the mentally handicapped persons from home to place of service delivery and back, home visit programmes by mobile professionals, financial assistance to such children need to be covered under the home based training programme to alleviate the burden of family members in the optimal use of home care and management of individuals with mental handicap.

Some of the studies so far reviewed in this section reported no significant effect of burden which means individuals families vary in their coping strategies. It may be due to the impact of culture and close-knit nature of the traditional family system. The following review may help one to identify the various coping styles and strategies employed by the individuals in the families.

Number of authors have studied families overtime and looked at different ways in which families cope with stress wither by coming closer together or moving farther apart. Minuchin (1967) distinguished the movement towards either cohesiveness or greater distance from one another as enmeshment or disengagement.

Folkman et al., (1979) viewed coping as "efforts", both action-oriented and intra-psychic to manage environmental and internal demands and conflicts among them, which tax or exceed a person's resources. These coping resources vary across time and also vary in the degree to which persons can utilize them at a given time, subject to different coping demands.

Lazarus and his colleagues have outlined five broad categories of coping resources (Folkman et al., 1979);

1. Health/Energy/Morals.
2. Problem solving skills.
3. Social networks (actual and perceived social support systems).
4. Utilitarian resources (SES, money, available community programmes and agencies).

5. General and specific beliefs (Belief about self efficacy, faith in God, fate or some higher natural order.

Family coping was defined by McCubbin et al., (1980) as the group's management of a stressful event or situation by the family as a unit with no detrimental effects on any individual in the family. Family coping according to Boss (1988) is the cognitive, effective and behavioural process by which individuals and the family system as a whole manage rather than eradicate stressful events or situations.

Friedrich et al., (1985) used a multidimensional and longitudinal frame work for studying coping resources and adjustment in families with a child who has mental retardation. A sample of one hundred and forty (140) mothers of mentally retarded children whose age ranged from 3 to 19 years were the respondents. It was hypothesized that four dimensions of coping resources; utilitarian, health/energy/morale, social support and belief systems as well as child characteristics would predict parenting outcome as measured by Factor I Parent and Family Problems of QRS-F. The focus in this study was the child characteristics which were divided into two variables; one, medical involvement which was closely associated with severity of the disability; the other, medical problems including both internalizing and externalizing behaviour.

Results of regression analysis indicated that three of the four categories of coping resources were significant contributors of additional variance beyond that of behavioural and physical problems of the child. For validational purposes one hundred and four (104) mothers of the original sample were re-examined 10 moths later. The original analysis was supported and changes in marital satisfaction were related to an increase in parent and family problems over the elapsed time span. The data from this study clearly indicated the importance of a variety of sources in the coping process.

Cole (1986) provided a theoretical framework for understanding the relation between family stressors, family resources and child placement. In-home versus out-of-home placement is regarded as one index of family adaptation. Stressors related to the child's handicapping condition combine with the family's pre-existent stressors to produce crisis. Faced with excessive demands, the family may cope by eliminating the stressor which is nothing but placing the child out-of-home.

Cole and Meyer (1989) conducted a study to find out the impact of needs and resources on family plans to seek out-of-house placement. Parents with severely retarded children living at home were surveyed with regard to those variables and their plans for future child placement. Multiple regression analysis revealed that child related stressors were negatively related to parent's plans for keeping the child at home until the age of twenty one years and positively related to plans for placing the child outside the home before the age of twenty one years. Families with high levels of internal resources are more apt to report plans for keeping the child at home indefinitely. Degree of external resources use was related to plans to maintain the child at home until the age of twenty one years, over and above both child related stressors and family resources.

Tung and Jagijit (1994) conducted a study to see the sex differences on a measure of coping strategies. Two hundred (200) students (100 male and 100 female) were studied using the coping operations preference enquiry (Schutz., (1978). Statistical analysis of the data through "t" test showed significant differences between the two groups. The males used the coping styles of "Denial" (a coping style in which the individual denies of having any stress) and "Isolation (a tendency to be less emotional and face the situation more intelligently). Females were significantly high on turning against self—a pattern in which the individual is fully aware of the stressful events but considers herself incompetent to face it and holds oneself responsible for it.

Family stress, family burden and coping styles adapted by families of mentally retarded children may directly or indirectly affect the functioning of the family. This may interfere with the individual's adjustment as well as satisfaction which go a long way in raising a mentally handicapped child.

Studies Related to the Influence of Mentally Handicapped Child on Family Functioning

The term "family functioning" is not very clear though many synonymous terms such as "family strength" (Otto, 1963) "family homeostates" (Jackson, 1959), "family environment" (Moos and Moos, 1976), "family integration" (Farber, (1959), "energized family" (Prat, 1976), "family competence" (Lewis et al., 1976) and "social functioning of families" (Gerson, 1967) are used by researchers.

The overall meaning of the term "family functioning" is carrying out of family related roles. Poor family functioning indicates that relatively few of the tasks assigned to or expected of the family members are in fact being carried out. Hobart (1983) stated that family functioning is a dynamic concept relating to the way family members interact and carry out tasks. More specifically it is the process of fulfilling activities which contribute to the maintenance of the family unit and the well-being of its members.

The following are some of the definitions used in family research for the term "family functioning". Geismar et al., (1959, 1962, 1964) defined 'family functioning' as all behaviour including attitudes and feelings bearing upon well-being of the family group, which include, (a) all individual behaviour and adjustment of family members, (b) performance of roles in keeping with family role expectations of the community.

Deykin (1972) defined "family functioning" as behaviour and perception patterns among family members and between the family unit and the community.

Roghmann et al., (1973) defined family functioning as the successful meeting of necessary needs in the family.

Pless and Salterwhite (1973, 1975) interpreted family functioning as the way in which the family unit operates across many dimensions encompassing the dynamics of everyday life.

Lewis et al., (1976) defined the term as family competence, family with flexible structure, open to growth and change responsible to new stimulation and development of capable individuals.

Smilkstein (1978), Delvecchio Good et al., (1979) Young Chen et al., (1980) stated family functioning as the process of nurturing that promotes emotional and physical growth and maturation of family members.

Kaplan et al., (1978) viewed it as fulfillment of role responsibilities.

Olson (1979) defined family functioning as family member's perception of family cohesion and adaptability.

Goldenberg and Goldenberg (1980) state that family is far more than a collection of individuals occupying a specific physical and psychological space together. Rather it is a natural social system with properties all its own, one that has evolved a set of roles, a power structure, form of communication and ways of negotiation and problem solving that allow various tasks to be performed effectively.

These tasks that the family performs are referred to as the functions or outputs of the family system. By carrying out its functions the family shares the common goal of serving the collective and individual needs of its members.

The family systems framework identifies nine specific functions that families typically perform (Turnbull, Summers and Bortherson, 1983)—economic, physical, rest and recuperation, socialization, self-definition, affection, educational, vocational and guidance.

A non-normative change like the birth of a handicapped child that a family may experience, is a functional change. Functional change results in a shift in the way in which a family carries out its various functions. In many families children are expected to take on increasing responsibility for caring for themselves as they grow older and for contributing to the needs of the household. However, this is not true of families with severally handicapped members.

The term family functioning has often been used interchangeably with family coping and family adaptation (Reiss et al., 1980) and family cohesion and adaptability (Olsen, 1979). Family coping and family functioning may probably mutually affect each other.

Pelz et al., (1984) state that good family functioning can be indicated by individual member's satisfaction with expressive activities.

Assessment of the functioning of families of retarded children as a unit is the area that has received the least attention. However, there are a few studies which need to be mentioned. Some such studies conducted in this area are reported in the following paragraphs.

Kershener (1970) compared family functioning in two groups of homes; in one group the mentally retarded child was kept at home while in the other child was institutionalized. Information was collected through parent interviews and follow-up interviews were conducted a year later to obtain an estimate of the effect on the two groups of families over time. The quality of family functioning was rated in a number of areas; home and household practices, economic practices, social activities, health and health practices, care and training of children, family relationships and family unity and individual behaviour and adjustment. As predicted, the level of functioning increased over the year interval for the families that institutionalized the child and decreased for those that kept the child at home.

Since a mentally retarded child is a source of family stress, institutionalization is one way in which a family attempts to cope with that stress and according to Kershner study this solution is successful in alleviating some of the family tensions.

Hurder (1973) in an UNESCO (Paris) report mentioned that sociological studies on the effect of severely mentally retarded children on family integration increased. Findings included the observation that severely retarded boys were much more disruptive to the home than girls, that older sisters are more apt to suffer restrictions due to the severely retarded child than the boys and that severely retarded children are most disruptive to families in the higher socio-economic bracket.

A critical review of research on vocational and community adjustment stressed the need for more refined description and analysis of the behavioural characteristics of the retarded, better analysis of family variables and sharper criteria of vocational success.

Research on the family increased in amount and variety but was generally inconclusive. Typical of this research was comparison of various types of family counselling, study of the effect of the retarded child's participation in classes for the TMR on parental attitude and evaluations of family dynamics as a function of placement of the child in a residential facility versus retaining at home.

Begab and Richardson (1975) observed that trauma of having

a retarded child presents a serious disruptive force to the family life style.

Pratt (1976) has described families who cope with stressful events as those who are characterized by flexible role relationships and shared power. Resources must be allocated among multiple goals to meet the needs of the family and satisfy relationships.

McCubbin et al., (1980) suggested that when it is the family unit rather than an individual who is dealing with a stressful event or problem the same resources are potentially available both to the individuals within the family and to the family as a group. The family system's internal resources, namely, cohesion and adaptability need to be considered in this context.

Nihira et al., (1980) studied 268 families of educable and trainable mentally retarded children (EMR and TMR) living at home using numerous measures of the home environment, family adjustment and child characteristics. The results indicated that family adjustment and functioning were related not only to the severity of the child's retardation and degree of mal-adaptive behaviour but to family demography characteristics, the psycho-social climate of the home (e.g. family cohesion, expressiveness and harmony) and specific kinds of parental behaviour towards their retarded children. In addition the perceived impact was related to marital disharmony, family conflict and maladaptive behaviour of the retarded child.

The investigators have also demonstrated the interaction and reciprocal nature of the family-retarded child system as the parents' feelings of the impact were related to the retarded children's lack of adaptive competency and the children's adaptive competency was related to the parent's successful coping with the problem of mental retardation. The study suggested both the difficulties these families face as well as the variability of this impact within groups of families with retarded children.

Nihira et al., (1980) studied the relationships between home environment, family adjustment and the social competency of mentally retarded children. The subjects were one hundred and fourteen (114) TMR (Trainable Mentally Retarded) children and one hundred and fifty two (152) EMR (Educable Mentally Retarded) children. The subjects (about half male and half female in each group) had a mean I.Q. of 42.4 with the standard deviation of 9.9 for the TMR group and a mean I.Q. of 66.4 with the standard deviation of 10.0 for the EMR group. All children resided in their natural homes with married parents.

The variables employed in the study are : (a) parental behaviour and attitude towards the child, (b) psychological climate of the family, (c) demographic and structural description of home, (d) family adjustment and (e) character of the child.

Results indicated that there are significant differences in the socio-economics status, TMR families being higher than EMR. The number of children is some what larger in EMR homes than in TMR homes. The degree of impact on family appears to be greater for TMR than for EMR groups. However, the parental attitude towards the impact is found to be higher i.e., more positive attitude in the TMR homes than in the EMR homes. The Family Environment Scale indicated that TMR families are more cohesive and have less conflict than EMR families.

The adaptive behaviour scale data indicated that EMR children are significantly higher than TMR children in these factors of adaptive behaviour. However, the EMR children appear to have more maladaptive behaviour than TMR children.

The following conclusions were drawn from the results of the above study :

1. An educationally stimulating home environment is associated with adaptive competence of the children in both groups.
2. Social adjustment (Vs maladaptive behaviour) of the children is related to cohesiveness and harmony (Vs disorganization and conflict) at home.
3. An educationally stimulating home environment for the TMR children depends primarily upon the quality of parenting and child rearing practices.
4. An educationally stimulating home environment for the EMR children involves psycho-social climate of home as well as culturally stimulating atmosphere and educational expectations.

5. Family harmony and quality of parenting are related to the family's ability to cope with the problem of mental retardation.

6. The family is likely to feel that the mentally retarded has major impact on the family especially when there are other family conflicts.

7. The feeling of impact is also related to maladaptive behaviour of the child.

These conclusions formed the basis for framing questions for experimental verification in the present study.

In a later study Mink et al., (1983) using some of the same subjects utilized a cluster analytic approach to create a typology of family life styles. The five clusters identified clearly underscore the heterogeneity of families with a mentally retarded child. they were cohesive-harmonious, control-oriented-inharmonious, child-oriented-expressive disadvantaged low morale, and low disclosure-inharmonious. The investigators speculated that the differences among clusters were possibly due to differential availability of support systems.

Another study by the same investigators to the inter-relationships of home environment and school adjustment of TMR children revealed that family harmony and cohesiveness, quality of parenting, emotional support for learning and cognitive stimulation available at home were significantly related to the child's school adjustment. These results suggest that familial coping within a specific home environment influences the retarded child's adaptation in a related ecological context. Although Nihira et al., 91981) focused on a child outcome, several investigators have shown that social relationships and support available from several sources has a positive impact on parental functioning (Farber, 1959; Friedrich, 1979; Friedrich and Friedrich, 1981).

Ishtiag and Kamal (19810 studied 20 moderately retarded children and their families. Results indicated that seventy two (72%) per cent of the families had marital disharmony as a result of birth of handicapped child. About 56 per cent of parents had a negative attitude, 88 per cent of the mentally retarded children were neglected by their parents.

Reiss (19810 in a series of experiments with over a thousand (1000) families found that families manage self-regulation within certain parameters and take on different aspects of one another's functioning in order to protect the "balance" of the family as a whole.

Agathanos and Vales (1982) studied 88 families with a Mongol child between the ages of 4–14 years. The information was collected through home interviews focusing on two areas (a) general characteristics which comprised the objective situation of the families, family structure, ages, education, child condition, socio-economic class; and (b) the effect on the family. The second area was sub-divided into sub-areas; the effect on the siblings, the relationship of father to the child and the effect on total family functioning.

Five years later all families that could be traced were interviewed in order to see any possible change or any new problem emerging since most of the children had entered into adolescence. Forty Nine families were interviewed as the others were not found.

Results indicated that 35 per cent of the mothers who were graded as "seriously affected" by the Mongol child feel lonely, depressed, guilty and avoided every outing, fearing comparison of their child with normal children. Both their physical as well as mental health are affected.

Forty four per cent of the mothers rated as "fairly affected" were more realistic and have been making efforts to adjust to the problem and plan for the future. A few mothers found in this child's company, pleasure and no burden at all.

With regard to the aspect of family functioning, Down's syndrome families presented a lower level of family life when compared with the control group. The most significant finding was the difference within the same group among families with the same objective situation. The personality of the mother and other children and secondly the degree of child's handicap interfered with the family functioning.

The follow-up study results demonstrated an improvement in 80 per cent of the children as per their mother's description.

Dybwad (1982) expressed that physicians, social workers and

psychologists were convinced that the mere presence of a mentally handicapped child in a family would prove detrimental to other siblings and constitute an unbearable burden to the parents. The situation seems to be tense primarily because parents were left without services, without guidance and without emotional support of any kind.

Balachandran (1985) in an article on the role of family in the promotion of mental health of its members clearly emphasized the performance of some family functions serve as support system to its members. The case study presented in the article reemphasized the potential that exists within a family unit that can be relied upon to restore and strengthen the individual.

Puri and Sen (1989) opined that the behaviour of mentally handicapped child was disruptive to the smooth functioning of any group whether in the family or in the play-ground or in the class room and could prevent the child's integration in such groups. The reaction of the group members to such disruption might be one of the rejection, exclusion, punishment or the disorganisation of the group itself.

Shulman et al., (1990) studied the impact of mentally retarded child on the family system as a whole and on the rules and structures that govern transactions among family members. More specifically the study attempted to identify the "family system" of families with a mentally retarded child using the typology suggested by Reiss (1981).

Reiss (1981) found three main dimensions to characterize family interaction during problem solving; (1) configuration, (2) Co-ordination and (3) Closure.

Configuration is the contribution of family in enhancing problem solving when the entire family works as a group.

Coordination refers to the tendency and capacity of the family members to solve problems in the same manner.

Closure represents the degree to which the family defers its final solution until all its members have collected all the information they can obtain conceptually. Configuration exemplifies the family's effective adaptability to new situations. Coordination connotes the importance which the family gives to cohesion and cooperation, and closure pertains to the family's level of flexibility using these dimensions. Reiss suggested a family typology consisting of three main types of families. The three consensual family types reflecting the level and role of consensus in the family, one effective and the other two faulty.

The sample consisted of 39 families of trainable mentally retarded children from the greater Tel Aviv area in Israel. Twenty two had children (13 boys and 9 girls) who studied in schools for moderately mentally retarded children. Seventeen children (13 boys and 4 girls) who were also moderately retarded but in addition exhibited disruptive behaviour studied at a special school for behaviourally disordered and mentally retarded children.

The children ranged in age from 6–17 for the moderately retarded first group (N = 128) S.D. was found to be 2.93 while for the retarded and behaviourally disruptive group (N = 129) S.D. was found to be 2.90. The I.Q. range for children in both the groups was from 25 to 50 with no differences between the two groups.

All the families participating in the study were intact families (father's mean age was 42.3 and S.D. = 5.7 and mother's mean age was 38.2 with S.D. = 5.6). Parents' mean education was 10 years of schooling with S.D. = 3.5. There was no significant difference between ages and education of the parents of the children in the two different schools.

The families were classified into family types according to parents' performance on the Reiss card – Sort procedure. Results revealed that there is not significant relationship between the type of faulty family and the severity of behavioural children's disorders. (X^2=2.16, $P < 0.05$).

Some attempts have been made by investigators to study the inter-relationship between the stress produced with a handicapped child in the family and its functioning.

Dyson (1991) investigated the differences between families with children with special needs and those with children without special needs with regard to stress and family functioning. Fifty five (55) families with young children with handicaps were compared with a matched group of families of children without handicaps. Instruments used for the study were questionnaire on Resources and Stress, Short Form (QRS–F) Friedrich, Greenberg and Crnic, 1983) and the Family Environment Scale (Moos and Moos, 1981).

Results indicated that parents of children with handicaps scored substantially higher on QRS–F scale than parents of children without handicaps on each of the measures. The two groups did not differ on any domain of the family social environment. The results provided strong evidence that family stress is related to the care of a child with special needs, in middle class families.

The results of step-wise multiple regression analysis indicated that the best predictor of parental stress was the presence of handicap accounting for 41 per cent of the variance. The other significant predictor was family relationship with a variance of 6 per cent.

The results provide strong evidence that family stress is related to the care of a child in middle class families. Families of special needs children showed a distinct style of functioning along family dimensions. These families emphasized achievement and moral religious beliefs and valued set rules and procedures for operating family life more than families who do not have children with handicaps.

The results further suggest that a child with handicaps may have differential effects on various family psychological dimensions and parental stress is not necessarily predictive of family dysfunctioning. This finding supports a competence model in which families may respond to the care of a child with handicaps with resilience and adaptive functioning. Special consideration needs to be given to identifying factors protecting families from the potentially negative impact of raising such children.

Another attempt was made by Dyson in (1993) to study parental stress and family functioning over time in families of children with disabilities. Seventy four (74) of the hundred and ten (110) families in the original study (Dyson, 1991) have participated in this study. Thirty eight (38) families were from the disability group because of the presence of disability in their children and thirty six families were from the non-disabled group because of absence of disability in their children. Same instrument as in the first study were used for the collection of information. Results showed a higher level of stability in parental stress and a modest degree of consistency over time in family functioning in families of children with disabilities.

In these aspects, families of children with disabilities were not different from comparison families. There was also stability in the best predictors of parental stress (presence or presence of disabilities and the quality of family relationship). Families of children with disabilities were distinguished by the exceedingly greater amount of stress at both periods of study.

Cullen et al., (1991) investigated the variables influencing the functioning of families with mentally retarded persons. Sample consisted of 62 families with mentally retarded persons living at home in various stages of the life cycle. The age groupings were based on the chronological age of the person with MR as follows: (1) Infancy (0–2), (2) Pre-school (3–6), (3) School age (7–10), (4) Early adolescence (11–14), (5) Late adolescence (15–21) and (6) Adulthood (22–53).

Three instruments used in the study were Family adaptability and Cohesion Evaluation Scales to measure family functions and satisfaction. The family crisis oriented Personal Evaluation Scale was used to measure family coping process. A sub-scale of the Chronicity Impact and Coping Instrument, Parent Questionnaire (CICI; PQ) was used to measure the perceived family stressors or concerns. Results demonstrated the importance of some fathers' characteristics to maternal coping skills in two parent households. Although mean maternal coping scores were not statistically different between two parent and single parent households, single mother's coping skills showed strong negative association with both the number of children in the household and the age of the mother. This was not true of mothers in two parent households. Single parent mothers also appeared to be considerably more dissatisfied with family functioning, than mothers in two parent households. The supportive role of older fathers in mother's coping in two parent households also was apparent. The implications of this study point to the need for greater support for mothers of young children with MR, mothers who are sole care-givers and parents with many children.

Saetermore et al., (1991) conducted a validation study in order to assess the content, construct and criterion related validities of the Parenting Style Survey, an instrument assessing parental behaviour in families with a child who has mental retardation.

Subjects were the primary care-providers of twenty nine (29) individuals with moderate or severe mental retardation. The children ranged in age from 16–22 years.

Family visits by the researchers during dinner time were used for the study. The primary care-provider filled out the Parenting Style Survey and Family Environment Scale immediately following dinner.

The researchers demonstrated adequate levels of reliability and validity for the seven dimensions comprising the Parenting Style Survey. The seven dimensions are power assertion, Love withdrawal, Induction, Control Maturity, Demands, Autonomy and Nurturance. Parenting Style Survey is an easily administered instrument that provides useful information regarding the behaviours a parent uses when dealing with a child with mental retardation.

Koller et al., (1992) presented a comprehensive view of families of children with mental retardation from an epidemiological perspective. Data covered a 15 year period on the health, behaviour and functioning of a representative population of families of children with mental retardation and a comparison group children were used.

Cluster analysis included 157 families of children with mental retardation and 165 families of comparison children. Results indicated that only a small minority of families of children with mental retardation did not cluster together with comparison families. More than a third functioned well and had a middle class orientation while less than a third functioned poorly. A few clusters had ambiguous configuration, but most were easily understood and conformed generally to expectations in validation analysis.

The families which functioned well had children with lower I.Q.s than did children in other clusters, whereas the dysfunctional families had high rates of instability and possible or probable genetic pedigree. The children in dysfunctional families often had behavioural disturbance and although their I.Q.s spanned a large range in general, they had mild mental retardation.

The highest rate of behaviour disturbance in children with mental retardation occurred in families in clusters where rates of psychiatric disturbances were high for mothers or both parents.

In clusters where psychiatric disturbance was high for fathers only, behaviour disturbances were less frequent among children. Some of the clusters had unexpected configurations. Child loss was highest in the two clusters in which families of children with mental retardation predominated. The investigators at the end stated that since cluster analysis has limitations, it should be used selectively and interpreted with caution.

Hodapp and Zigler (1993) compared the families of children with severe mental retardation or autism and families of children without mental retardation taking Birenbaum and Cohen studies. Considering the needs of families with severe mental retardation or autism the following six solutions were proposed :

i) Looking at health care needs more broadly.

ii) Promoting the family as the unit receiving health services.

iii) Initiating programmes for young adults with serious chronic conditions in the after school years.

iv) Promoting simplicity in administering services.

v) Expanding the use of Medicaid to promote home and community based services.

vi) Providing financial supports to parents.

The authors at the end commented that some of these problems are though common with normal children they are magnified many times throughout many more years when caring for a child with mental retardation. Additional help need to be provided to such families to avoid making families of children with handicaps into "handicapped families".

Commenting on Birenbaum and Cohen's recommendations Mink (1993) opined that the shift of service delivery from the individual with disabilities to the family may adversely affect the individual. But the author reiterates that the shift in focus is not meant to diminish the needs of the individual who has developmental disabilities but rather to recognize the context in which the person lives. If the family is considered as a unit–as a functioning system, what affects one family member will affect all members. If the needs of the individual with developmental disabilities are being met to the exclusion of the needs of other family members, then the family as a whole suffers and the individual with disabilities also suffers.

In this connection Rowitz (1992) has noted that "mental retardation is a family affair" and what is in the best interests of the family is generally in the best interests of the individual with developmental disabilities.

Stanton (1992) has emphasized that the family unit must be seen as people interacting with in a context, both affecting it and being affected by it. Consequently family focused interventions assure that family members can change and family paradigms may be modified thus allowing new behaviours and family patterns of functioning to emerge, if the overall family context is changed.

Wells and Whittington (1993) examined the functioning of children and families treated in an intensive family preservation service programme. Study subjects were forty two (42) adolescent children and one of their parents. Data were collected from three sources–children, parents, and care workers. Subjects were studying at admission, at discharge and between 9 and 12 months after discharge. Data were drawn from semi-structured interviews and included four standardised measures viz., Family Assessment Device–Version 3 (FAD–McMaster Family Assessment Device, 1983), Interaction Behaviour Questionnaire (IBQ), Child Behavioural Check-list (CBCL and Youth Self Report (YSR). Univariate and multivariate analysis revealed that at follow up children and their families were functioning at a lower level than non-clinical samples, their functioning improved between admission and discharge and did not decline between discharge and follow up. Child and family factors were more strongly associated with family functioning at follow up than were treatment factors.

Another attempt was made by Nihira et al., (1994) who conducted home interviews with one hundred and two (102) families of children with developmental delays to assess eco-cultural family resources and constraints, values and goals as well as pro-active adaptive efforts to deal with their circumstances. Interview topics included (a) economic factors, (b) child safety, (c) domestic and child care workloads, (d) familial support networks and (e) socio-cultural influences.

Results indicated that some of the eco-cultural factors were unique and statistically independent of the traditional measures of home environment (e.g. child-rearing attitudes, cognitive stimulation of the child and general psycho-social climate) significant relations were found between certain eco-cultural factors like (a) the family's attempt to seek information and services for the child with developmental delay, (b) the amount of help available in the family, and (c) the career and work orientation of the parents and child's developmental status. Both eco-cultural factors and traditional family measures accounted for significant variation in child outcomes.

The extent to which the families attempt to seek information and utilize services, the amount of help available within the family and away from family (internal/external resources) may have a direct/indirect bearing on parental marital relationship and parent child interactions.

Parents' Marital Relationship and Mentally Handicapped Child

It is logical to think that if stress is associated with parenting a handicapped child the marital relationship will be vulnerable to the effects of that increased stress as well.

The marriages of the parents of retarded have not been systematically researched. Whatever little is done, has actually focused only on the issues of relative divorce rate and marital satisfaction rather than other issues such as communication, decision making and role flexibility (Sabbeth and Leventhal, 1984). Farber (1959) concluded that although marital satisfaction declined with the presence of a severely retarded child, out-come was more strongly related to the marital satisfaction of the parents prior to the child's birth. Parents with high satisfaction early in the marriage seemed to do better than those whose satisfaction had been initially lower. Sex of the child was also important to marital satisfaction as retarded male children had a more significant negative impact on the marriage.

Farber (1968) presents evidence of the adverse effects of mentally retarded child on marital integration, social activities, job promotion, family roles and sibling occupational expectations.

Rutter et al., (1970) stated that the presence of retarded child in the family brought about frequent quarrels between the parents.

Srivastava et al., (1975) assessed the attitudes of mothers of mentally retarded children and found that the mothers fostered dependency in children. Marital conflict, strictness with children, easy irritation with children, suppression of aggression and avoidance of communication were some of the trends observed in families with retarded children.

In several recent studies, investigators have assessed marital relationship with the Locke-Wallace Marital Adjustment Inventory (Locke and Wallace, 1959) with conflicting results. Friedrich and Friedrich (1981) comparing, matched groups of mothers of handicapped and non-handicapped children fond a significant difference in marital satisfaction with the former group reporting lower satisfaction. Using multiple regression to predict stress scores of 98 mothers of handicapped children Friedrich (1979) found that marital satisfaction which alone accounting for 33 per cent of the total variance, was the most significant predictor.

In contrast, Waisbern (1980) found no differences in marital satisfaction between two groups of well matched couples, half of whom were parents of developmentally delayed infants. Kazak and Marvin (1984) using Dyadic Adjustment Scale (Sanier, 1976) between two larger groups, one of which was composed of parents who had a child with spina bifida. The conflicting results of the three studies may be attributable to sample differences as the children in the Friedrich study averaged 9.8 years of age as opposed to 7.5 years in Kazak's study and 13 months in the Waisbern's report.

The variability in the findings on marital satisfaction suggests that marital response is not uniform and may be dependent upon factors other than the presence of a retarded child. Such factors may be the severity of the handicap, the age and sex of the child and the quality of the marital relationship prior to the presence of the child.

Friedrich and Friedrich (1981) reported that in comparison with families of non-handicapped children, families of handicapped children were found to have less satisfactory marriages, less social support, less religious affiliation and less psychological well being.

A comparative study of the family conditions of normal and retarded children by Biswas (1980) indicated that the marital relationship among the parents of retarded in major numbers were found to be unhealthy as compared to that of normal children.

Family Interaction and Mentally Handicapped Child

The available literature on families of mentally retarded children suggested that the parents and siblings of retarded children individually as well as the family as a whole are at-risk for numerous difficulties in comparison to families with non-retarded children.

Studies of parent-retarded child interaction can be categorized as : (a) analysis of mother-child linguistic patterns and (b) studies of responsiveness and communications styles in mother-child interaction.

Mother's speech to their retarded children has received the most attention, with conflicting results. In the initial study Marshall et al., (1973) measured the frequency of verbal operands during interactions between 20 mothers and their retarded children and 20 mothers with their non-retarded children matched for CA. The non-retarded children used more and varied verbal operands and mothers of retarded children used more commands.

Several subsequent investigators with more appropriate controls have reported either minimai group differences (Buckhalt, Rutherford and Goldberg, 1978, Gutman and Rondal, 1979) or no differences at all (Rondal, 1978).

Several interaction studies measuring responsiveness and communication between groups of mothers with retarded and non-retarded children have yielded meaningful differences. Kogan et al., (1969) compared a group of 6 retarded children and their mothers with a control group of 10 mother non-retarded child pairs on parameters of relative status, affection and involvement. Mothers of retarded children displayed extreme degrees of warmth and friendliness less frequently. The retarded children generally displayed a more neutral status (neither dominant nor submissive).

Several subsequent investigators measuring interactive behaviour during free play and structured situations (Breiner and Forehand, 1982; Vitze, Abernathy Asha and Faultstich, 1978) have found a general synchrony in the interactive behaviour of mother-retarded child dyads. Mothers of retarded children tend to be more active and directive with their children. Retarded children were found to be both less responsive and less complaining to their mothers than were non-retarded children.

The interactive patterns of mother-retarded child pairs suggest difficulties in the reciprocity within the relationship, Vitze et al., (1978) found that developmentally delayed infants vocalization were not contingent on maternal speech as were the vocalizations of non-delayed infants.

Similar findings were reported by Cunningham et al., (1981) and Terdal et al., (1976) with older retarded children responding less contingently to maternal social behaviour than did non-retarded mental age matched children.

Floyd and Phillipe (1993) in a study compared the in-home interactions of mothers and fathers with their school age children with mild and moderate mental retardation (n=53) and children without mental retardation (n=51).

The parents completed a battery of questionnaires that included the demographic variables like child adjustment, parenting attitudes, social support and psychological distress along with other measures of family relationships. The family also participated in a series of videotaped interaction tasks. Typical activities included preparing dinner eating and cleaning up afterwards and baking cookies or family crafts. The child's primary school teacher's assessment of child's psycho-social adjustment and behaviour problems at school were considered.

The results indicated that the parents of children with mental retardation were relatively more controlling and less playful with their child. However, they also employed affective behaviour management practices without resorting to coercive control strategies. Further 24–51 per cent of the variance in interaction processes were predicted by a set of risk factors common to both groups namely behaviour problems of the child, authoritarian parental attitudes, poor social support for the parents and parental depression. The status of the child as having or not having mental retardation accounted for relatively little unique variance.

Researchers have recently begun to address the role of fathers of children with disabilities which often costs the father as peripheral to the child's development. Tallman (1965) stated that the relative lack of involvement of fathers with their disabled children is due to their inability to cope with the situation. Gallager, Beckman and Cross (1983) explained this as the father's discomfort with the female dominated service systems. Bristol, Gallagher and Schopler (1988) opined that because of role differentiation between parents, fathers roles do not often include direct child care.

Some researchers have reported the fathers role negatively. Fathers of children with disabilities are less likely be playmates of their child than are fathers of children without disabilities. Bristol et al., (1988) McConachie (1989) and Parke (1988) have consistently shown that child care activities are not roles that fathers of children with disabilities ordinarily hold. Fathers spend less time in direct child care activities than mothers.

Studies have mainly concentrated on time use among parents of children with disabilities and exclusively focused on direct child care activities (McConachie, 1989; Stoneman, Brody and Abbott, 1983; Smith, 1986). Although direct child care is certainly of great importance there has been little study of other categories of time use by fathers or children with disabilities.

Family's function as a socializing agent and as Skrtic et al., (1984) point out, that a handicapped child may have differential effects upon siblings socializing experiences. One sibling may experience reduced social interactions because of care-taking responsibilities for a handicapped sibling or because of peer rejection whereas another sibling may benefit from the teaching skills and positive attitudes learnt as part of growing up with a handicapped family member.

Normal siblings in the family perceive and adjust to mental retardation in the family in ways similar to those of their parents. Their parents offer a model to them of how to respond to the mentally retarded (Grossman, Schrieber and Feeley, 1965; Begab 1968).

Studies of families with a mentally handicapped child indicate that when parents were not stressed the siblings were adapting well. Nevertheless, the adolescent normal sibling is reportedly at increased risk for stress. This risk is related to the burden of care on the family of raising a mentally retarded child (Grossman, 1972; Gath, 1974; Ruseman, 1981).

Fowle (1968) stated that the resentment of added child care responsibility has been cited as a cause of tension between mothers and non-handicapped daughters.

Klein (1972 a) reported that sibling of a retardate had resented the responsibility as an intrusion on their time. On the contrary Grossman (1972) reported that some siblings have found it to be an enriching experience.

Simmension and McHale (1981) noted in a review of literature that siblings of handicapped children are often well adjusted and characterized by maturity and a responsible attitude that goes beyond their age.

Meyer (1984) considers the siblings of a retarded as one who is at-risk or one whose developmental tasks are simply different. Research studies indicated that the normal sibling as a result of having a retarded brother or sister has difficulties in negotiating adaptive and developmental tasks and is in need of professional intervention.

Ramadevi (1991) in a study regarding the attitudes of rural children towards their mentally handicapped siblings indicated that majority of children favoured their retarded sisters to their retarded brothers.

This finding is consistent irrespective of the sex, age, ordinal position and educational level of siblings of retarded children.

Stoneman and Crapps (1990) studied the mentally retarded individuals in family care homes and their relationship with the family of origin. A sample of one hundred and four (104) home providers completed a set of questionnaires focusing on family visitation, client trips home and other forms of family contact. When combined predictors of family visitation were examined, the three variables contributing unique variance were, the participation of family in placement, the provider's encouragement of involvement and the living status of the father.

Another important finding of the study is that gender patterns occurred in sibling involvement. Brothers and sisters were equally likely to visit their mentally retarded siblings at the care home but when clients travelled they almost always went to visit sisters. Providers reported less stress when siblings visited more often and when residents were able to go home for visits suggesting that certain aspects of family involvement may act as a support for providers. It is unclear why visits from siblings but not parents related to lesser stress.

Brody et al., (1991) studied the interaction between children with mental retardation and their younger siblings without retardation as well as those of an equal number of comparison pairs without mental retardation.

The second objective of the study was to test hypothesis concerning the relation of the language and adaptive skills of the older children with mental retardation to the degree of asymmetry displayed in their sibling interactions. The hypothesis is that the greater adaptive and linguistic competence in older siblings with mental retardation is associated with more symmetrical sibling relationships, because more competent older siblings require less management help and teaching from the younger sibling who is not retarded.

Subjects were 64 children (32 sibling pairs), sixteen sibling pairs (8 of each gender) contained a child with mental retardation and a younger same sex sibling. Non-handicapped comparison sibling pairs were matched on the ages of older and younger siblings, sex, race, parents' education and family income. In addition, groups were matched on parental marital status, family size, sibling spacing (the number of years between the age of the younger and older sibling) and relative birth order.

A series of 2 (sibling group; pairs with and without a child who had mental retardation) into 2 (child gender) analysis of variance revealed no significant group differences on age of older or younger siblings, sibling spacing, birth order of the target siblings, family size, age or education of the mothers or fathers or family income.

The results of the study indicated the younger siblings of older children with mental retardation assumed dominant roles involving helping, teaching and behaviour management than did the younger siblings of children without mental retardation. The patterning of these results was also reflected in the sibling role asymmetry index analysis. Sibling pairs including a child with mental retardation evinced role asymmetries reflecting the younger siblings dominance whereas comparison siblings pairs were characterized by dominant older siblings.

No differences in affect were found between the sibling groups. The competence of the child with mental retardation reliably predicted sibling role asymmetries and the observational contexts influenced sibling behaviour in both groups. Gender differences in roles and behaviour were minimal.

Studies Related to Support Systems for the Families with Mentally Handicapped Children

Families in general are embedded in a set of informal and formal support systems that can significantly modify the interaction of family members and thereby often affect the developing child. A number of studies have suggested that their is a positive relationship between informal social networks and a family's adaptation to stressful events, such as divorce (Hetherington, Cox and Cox, 1982) and job loss (Bronfenbrenner and Cronter, 1982). In the case of families with retarded children social networks are particularly important aids to successful coping and adaptation. However, a number of studies have documented that these families are socially isolated (Birenbaum, 1970, Carver and Carver, 1972; Illingworth, 1967). In a study, McDowell and Gabel (1981) found significantly smaller social networks for parents of mentally retarded infants as compared to a contrast group of parents of normally developing infants. Finally, smaller networks or no network also may lead a family with mentally retarded infant to social isolation.

Social isolation in families of mentally retarded children is an often reported finding. (Carver and Carver, 1972; Davis and Mackay, 1973; Dunlop and Horlingsworth, 1977; Farber, 1959, 1960, 1964; Hold, 1958; Jacobs, 1974; Legaay and Keough, 1966; Lavinson 1975; McAllister et al., 1973; Mayerwitz and Farber, 1966; and Schonnel and Watts, 1956). The family seems to have a diminished circle of acquaintances and contacts, belongs to fewer organizations and shares fewer leisure time activities. The lack of integration into their community, the impoverished social life and a lack of vacation time deprive these families of intra and inter familial resources.

Davis (1967) reported that the maternal grandmother usually plays an important role in the life of the new family. Fifty families with retarded children were compared with 30 normal families in order to determine the support given by the maternal grandmother. Support is described as "intimate" if the maternal grandmother lives nearby and visits frequently; as "effective" when she is available on call; as "ineffective" when there is little or no contact and as "unfamiliar" when she is not available. Less than one-half of the families with a retarded child had "effective" support from the maternal grandmother. In contrast, the normal control families received "effective" support, three quarters or more of the time. The reason given for this findings probably lies in the quality of family's relationships which tended to be strained in those with a retarded child, rather than in geographical factors. In order to find out exact pattern of support and relationships, it may be necessary to focus the attention on the available support system models.

Caplan (1976) suggested a model of support systems which focus on the health promoting and ego fortifying effects of social aggregates. He observes that an individual's continuing interaction with another individual or group or organization can add to his abilities of coping with his environment.

The special attributes of such support systems lie in their acting as a "buffer against disease" by providing the individual with feed back about his environment, by being interested in him as a person and by respecting his unique needs.

However, there are studies which conclude support systems do not influence the extent of stress experienced by mothers of retarded children. One such study is reported below.

Bradshaw and Lawton (1978) assessed the relation of mother's level of stress to the social and economic circumstances of the family. It was concluded that little of the variation in the level of stress could be ascribed to the extent of social and physical conditions of the family and child and that the provision of goods, services or financial assistance did not appear to have an impact on the level of mental well being of the mothers. Thus the overall conclusion of the study was that neither the severity of the handicap nor tangible support service and external environmental conditions were significantly related to maternal stress associated with caring for a handicapped child.

But, Johnson and Sarason (1978) have reported that social support has a demonstrated buffering effect. High stress families with high social support cope better than do similarly stressed families with low social and low stress families do equally well with or without peer social support. The relationship is interactive in that better copers presumably have more social support and more social support facilitates coping.

The results of research about the influence of support system did not demonstrate clear-cut trends and are following a "not here and not there" pattern.

Friedrich (1979) found that social support was not significantly related to coping.

Silver and Wortman (1980) identified the presence of social support as one of the important variables influencing the individual's coping process. In the case of social support actual social support is less important than perceived social support because an individual may under-estimate or over-estimate support resources. Also the simple presence of social support is not helpful if the individual is unable or unwilling to use it.

Tucker (1982) reviewed literature indicating that it is the absence of support that interferes with adjustment and not the presence of support that facilitates it. Lazarus (1966) indicated that all relationships are not helpful. Lieberman (1982) commented that all stressful situations cannot be remedied with help from others and different sources of social support may be effective only at certain stages of the stress process.

Waisbern (1980) in a study comparing Danish and U.S. parents of disabled children found that the relationship between use of support systems and coping was a complicated one. Support from informal sources such as family was found to be related to positive feelings towards the child. Still the families experienced more symptoms of internal stress. Formal support services such as help from professionals or social agencies were not found to figure prominently in lessening the internal strain or facilitating positive adjustment to the birth of a developmentally disabled child. Waisbern further explained that support from family and friends correlated positively with an increase in the symptoms of stress as a trade-off. In order to relate better to their handicapped child, parents internalized some of the strain resulting in an increase in anxiety and physical symptoms of stress.

Wahler (1980) reported that mothers who did not profit from a parent training approach were characterized by insularity, that is they lived within sparsely constructed community social networks. These mothers differed in the functional nature of their social contacts as well. The type of support offered to these mothers tended to be directive and instructive, which was apt to be punishing to the insular mother.

Suelzle and Keenan (1981) studied the support networks utilized by parents of partially retarded children at four different stages over the life cycle. Parents of developmentally disabled children whose age ranged from 0–21 years life-cycle stages of child were pre-school, elementary, teenage and young adult. The following were the personal and professional supports explored :

- Manner in which parent found out that the child was developmentally disabled.
- Available extended family and community supports.
- Severity of disability.
- Manner of securing community service.
- Professional services utilized.
- Attitude towards direct service.
- Involvement in child's programme.
- Parent's organization.
- Opinions and public policy.
- Long term plans and objectives for child.

Results indicate that the type of health care professionals seen by family varies with life-cycle stage of child. Locating appropriate services differs by life-cycle stage. Pre-school parents rely on doctors and personal support. Parents of older children rely on school personnel. Utilization of personal support declines over life cycle.

Parents of older children are less supportive of normalization concept.

Apart from type of support, the agency which gives support seem to be of high value to the parents with mentally handicapped child. The following are the studies which report the extent of effect of persons rendering support on the amount of stress experienced by parents of mentally handicapped children.

German et al., (1982) studied social support and coping in familial with a mentally retarded child maintained at home. Support and help received from grandparents and extended family members was perceived as more valuable than from friends.

Beckman (1983) observed that friendship networks were significantly smaller for parents of mentally retarded children when compared with parents of normal children. However, family network sizes were equivalent and were more closely knit among parents of retarded children.

Kazak and Marvin's (1984) study reported that though the family support system fostered cohesiveness and support, it also generated stress as the avenues to other resources are limited.

The following are some of the studies which reviewed the influence of social support on the adjustment and coping system of parents of the mentally handicapped children.

Hammer (1983) described a model which explains the nature of the association between the social support and stressful life-events. Social networks are seen as providing feed back which confirms behaviour and maintains performance thereby contributing to better performance and good health. This model distinguishes between relatively small, dense, close knit networks and those which are more open with less inner-connections between individuals. It suggests that the more open set would tend not only to more diversity but to less secure mediation of feed back and access, while the more closed and dense set would tend to given more reliable mediation but with less flexibility and limited alternatives.

Cotterell (1986) studied ninety six (96) Australian working families in terms of how social support such as companionship, encouragement and useful advice influenced the quality of child rearing. The investigator concluded that the availability of social support was a powerful factor in improving the quality of child rearing. The investigator further expressed that the mother's social support network acts as "a buffer against the stressful intrusions of the work place into the family."

Alvey and Aeschleman (1990) designed a programme to train parents to teach their mentally retarded children age appropriate restaurant skills and evaluated. Families of three 7–9 year old children enrolled in a public school programme for moderately, mentally retarded children were recruited to participate in the experiment. Socio-economically all the three families were middle class. In all the three families, only the mothers of the handicapped children participated in the parent training programme and the restaurant probes.

The mothers were given a Parent Advice Manual describing general teaching procedures and specific instructions on how to generate ten (10) age appropriate fast food restaurant skills. Subsequently, a parent training session utilizing verbal instruction, modelling, role playing and descriptive feed back was conducted in each participant's home. The effectiveness of the training programme was evaluated by observing both parent and child performance during restaurant probes in which parent was instructed to teach the 10 targeted behaviours. The results indicated that the parent's teaching interactions were influenced by the training programme and that their children's restaurant skills were enhanced. The study provides an initial step toward the development of a technology for teaching age appropriate community living skills to developmentally delayed children.

Haldy et al., (1990) concluded that adequate social support had a positive influence on maternal feelings of competence about their child rearing abilities. Maternal satisfaction with help received by family members in caring for their child was positively correlated with feelings of competence. Mothers reported greater satisfaction with advice and services from various professionals when their child fell in milder mental retardation group.

Baker et al. (1991) studied the effects of parent training on families of children with mental retardation. Forty nine (49) families of children with mental retardation were assessed before and after a parent training programme on a variety of parent, marital and family measures. Parents reported high satisfaction with the programme and showed small but statistically significant decreases in reports of symptoms of depression, parent and family problems, overall family stress and dissatisfaction with the family's adaptability. The families that reported doing the least productive teaching had entered training reporting greater child related stress and lower satisfaction with the marriage and the family. The results suggested that the eventual success of parent training might be enhanced if programmes also intervene to enhance marital satisfaction or increase family adaptability or decrease stress—areas that are predictive of poorer long-term outcome.

Beckman (1991) reported that for both mothers and fathers of children with disabilities, increased informal support was significantly associated with decreased stress. Unlike informal support, formal support was not significantly associated with lower levels of stress. However, for fathers formal support was significantly negatively associated with general life stress.

Davis and Rushton (1991) evaluated a home-based, family focused counselling scheme providing support for English speaking and Bangladeshi families of children with intellectual or multiple disabilities. The sample for the study constituted fifty two (52) English speaking families (31 in intervention group and 21 in control group) and twenty eight (28) Bangladesh families (16 in intervention group and 12 in control group). Most families fell into the lower socio-economic range and many were unemployed.

All assessment procedures were carried out at home before and after intervention. Support questionnaire specifically devised for the study had seven point scales with a set of questions related to their perceived support and other ability to cope with the situation. Mothers rated on child grid about the disability, on parent grid about mothers constructions of themselves and their husbands and on relationship grid about mother's assessment of family relationships.

Malaise inventory was used as a measure of mother's stress/ emotional distress (Rutter et al., 1970).

Griffith's Mental Developmental Scale was used to assess children's developmental level (Griffth, 1970). Behaviour problems were assessed on the behaviour screening questionnaire (Rickman et al., 1982) modified by Cunningham (1987 b).

Results indicate that mothers and children in the intervention group showed significant and positive changes compared to randomly allocated controls. The greatest benefits were derived by the more deprived and initially less, well supported Bangladesh families. Mothers changed positively in ratings of perceived support and family functioning and in their constructions of their child, themselves, husbands and family relationships. Although systematic teaching was not included in the intervention programme their children also showed improvement in developmental progress and behaviour problems. The results strongly suggest that supportive counselling is an important element in working with families of children with disabilities.

Flynt et al., (1992) examined the perceived stress and the type and extent of social support utilized by mothers of children with mental retardation across the life cycle. Subjects were eighty (80) mothers of children who were developmentally delayed or diagnosed with moderate mental retardation. The children ranged in age from 6 months to 20 years. Mothers who agreed to participate were contacted by telephone and responded to the instruments utilized for the study. The two measures were the questionnaire on Resources and Stress Short Form (QRS-F) (Friedrich, Greenberg and Crnic, 1983) and the questionnaire on Social Support adopted by Crnic et al., (1984). The stress scale identified four independent factors; parent and family problems; pessimism, child characteristics and physical incapacitation. The social support scale measured the social support as a component of three factors—intimate relationships, friendships and community or neighbourhood support. Each item contains two parts, one addresses to the degree of support and the other pertains to the subject's satisfaction with the degree of support.

Results indicate that there were no significant differences in stress scores across the age groups. The perceptions of stress were stable for mothers of pre-schoolers through young adults. Significant differences were observed initially on utilization of social support by the mothers of pre-schoolers. However, when marital status was co-varied differences between groups were no longer significant. An analysis of the sub-scales of the questionnaire on social support showed that a significant difference existed between intimate relationships, friendships and community or neighbourhood supports for the mothers of pre-schoolers. An emerging trend suggests that mothers of pre-schoolers utilized social support to a greater extent than did mothers in the other two groups and these mothers relied more on intimate support than either friendship or community support networks.

Madhavan and Narayan (1992) studied the impact of professional intervention on the parental perceptions and expectations of their mentally retarded children. A semi-structured questionnaire with open ended questions was used to elicit perceptions and expectations. The questionnaire also included details on age, sex and level of retardation of the child and literacy level of parents and their locality of residence. One hundred parents whose children were followed up for atleast six months were included in the study. The perceptions and expectations of parents on their first visit were collected from the case records. The perceptions and expectations were elicited again during their follow up visit. The number of follow ups for each was noted.

The data on pre-intervention and post-intervention perceptions and expectations were grouped and analysed. Test of significant for difference of proportions was applied to each of the perceptions and expectations to find out the change. As can be seen from this description, this is not a perspective but a retrospective study.

Results indicated that from among ten major perceptions significant changes were noted in the areas regarding poor brain development as a cause for the condition ($P<0.01$) and the possibility of improvement in child with training. Out of 14 different expectations significant changes were noted in the areas of total cure, need for special education and speech development where the number asking for the former reduced ($P<0.01$) and those expecting training for the later increase ($P<0.01$, $P<0.05$).

Verma et al., (1992) evaluated home care programme for the mentally retarded children through training of the mother. Mothers of 80 children of mild (IQ 50–70) and moderate (IQ 35–49) mental retardation were selected for the study. A carefully developed home training programme was utilized to train half of the mothers, the other half forming the control group for the study.

The experimental and the control groups were matched for age and I.Q. of the children and age of the mothers. The women also did not differ significantly on the base line marital adjustment and parental attitude scores and the experienced social burden of the mothers. In the experimental group there was a significant increase in the I.Q. and improvement in the behaviour of the children and significant improvement in the marital adjustment scores, parental attitude and social burden felt by the mothers. There was no significant change in the control group in any of these variables. The results of this study give a ray of hope in reducing the hardships faced by the parents of the mentally retarded children with professional training.

Whatever positive attitudinal changes one might bring about in the parents through intervention, one should always remember that the quest or hope for a cure for the condition will always be present in a parent, though not consciously. So the professionals need to understand such feelings in a more balanced way and help the parents to set realistic goals for the future of their retarded children.

So, it has become the policy to concentrate on community based and home bound training or support type of intervention.

A number of models were advocated as support systems to the parents of mentally handicapped.

Peshawaria and Menon (1992) were optimistic in saying that parents and families are no doubt the biggest strength in India at present, though there are difficulties encountered while working with the families of children with mental handicap. Among the difficulties observed are financial burdens with no support from anywhere, large size of the families, misconceptions in parents regarding the condition of mental handicap, parental reliance on magical medical cures, and transportation problems in reaching available services.

Another problem parents face in our cultural set up, where guests are welcome anytime at home the parents are not able to carry out the programme at home due to this extra burden. Sometimes the over involvement and interference of neighbours and relatives, who suggest to parents methods of managing the child with mental handicap with other than systematic training leaves parents very confused.

The problem of both parents working with no extra support at home is posing a major challenge for parents of children with mental handicap and the service providers. Nevertheless, the strength of parents cannot be ignored and the fact that parents in India live and work for their children cannot be forgotten.

Girimaji (1993) over-viewed the family intervention in mental retardation and stated that home-based family care approach in mental retardation has gained world-wide recognition and research attention especially in the last two decades. She further states that there are clear advantages to the individual with mental retardation as well as to society in promoting family based care. However, there is a need to work with families to ensure optimum care as well as successful family adaptation. Approaches to such family interventions include; (a) parent education, (b) parent training, (c) parent counselling, (d) family social support networking and self-help groups and (e) transactional intervention.

According to Girimaji, the Indian researchers on the role of families with mental retardation had directed to the study of parents with an emphasis on parent's needs, parent's perception and attitudes. Very recently, a small but significant body of research work has emerged reporting different forms of family intervention. Brief inpatient family intervention model developed at NIMHANS in 1985 is worth mentioning in this context. This model could be considered as great support to parents of children with mental handicap. The model has been evolved to meet the needs of sub-groups of families who needed intensive intervention for reasons such as presence of high degree of stress and/or poor coping skills in the family following the birth of mentally handicapped child. However, the model seems to offer comprehensive care as it has been tailored to suit the needs of individual child and family.

However, Peshawaria and Menon (1993) described a working model developed at NIMH. This model includes a plan of working with parents in their families to strengthen their skills to promote parent involvement in various programmes. Other models tried at NIMH are as follows.

a) Institute based individual model wherein parents along with the child attend the services of the institute and initial assessment will be carried out by a multi-disciplinary team. Following the assessment, depending upon the needs of the child and the family, parents and other significant members are required to come along with the child on weekly basis to contact professionals for help. A management programme is designed by these professionals for the parents based on the specific needs of the child and family in order to carry out the programme at home. Children who are unable to get admission to special schools, benefit from such programmes since the focus is on both mentally handicapped child and family functioning.

b) The second model is institute based group activities where importance is given to child's learning. Small groups of six or seven children are involved. Parents of these children are encouraged to attend group activities along with the child.

c) Family Cottage : This was started at NIMH in order to help the outstation families for whom appropriate services may not be available in their setting.

   Facilities are provided to the family along with mentally handicapped child on temporary admission to family cottage for about 2–3 weeks. Here the focus is to promote both the child's learning as well as help to solve issues related to parents emotional needs and family functioning one a one-to-one basis.

d) Group Parent Training Programmes : This is done in order to encourage parents participation in training. A small group of thirty fathers and thirty mothers are encouraged to attend these programmes.

e) Sibling Groups : This approach is taken up to promote the involvement of siblings in the programme. Summer camps are conducted to the siblings of mentally handicapped children where they are trained to be aware of various needs and strengths of children with mental handicap.

All these models whether developed at NIMHANS or NIMH emphasize the need for creating awareness among family members about the needs of mentally handicapped and to improve their skills in order to provide better care to the mentally handicapped.

Over-View

The review of extensive literature available about family studies on mentally handicapped children has made it possible to make certain salient observations that would be used in proceeding further with the investigation of present problem. They are presented in the following paragraphs under separate headings.

Problems Faced by Parents of Mentally Handicapped Child

1. Families with mentally handicapped child have limited opportunities for social interactions.

2. Physical strain due to extra work involved in caring for a handicapped child and emotional stress are common in parents.

3. Burden of care is more, when the child is kept at home.

4. Parents are subjected to greater psychological stress in day-to-day management.

5. Parents often feel personally responsible for the mentally handicapped child's failures in social situations.

6. Severely retarded child's presence impedes the family development and places significant stress on the family unit.

7. Strain of caring for the handicapped child, readjustment of family's daily routine, additional time involved in caring for the child, the possibility of neglecting other family members and the difficulty to maintain harmony and integration in the family are common.

8. Father's special concerns with a mentally handicapped child are family budget, the cost of providing help for the child and academic success and whether the child will be able to support him/herself.

9. Social life of the parents of mentally handicapped child are adversely affected.
10. Financial burden was often reported by families with mentally handicapped child.
11. Behaviour problems associated with mental retardation impose extra care taking demands and burden on parents.
12. Mental retardates from rural and non-nuclear families posed fewer problems to the parents.
13. Misunderstandings, bickering among family members and marital disharmony were reported problems.
14. Parents feeling of burden, depended on the degree of retardation.
15. Child welfare issues and restrictive time demands were the most intense family problems, reported by mothers of retarded children.
16. Problems experienced by the parents of mentally handicapped child depend on the stage of the life cycle of the family.

Since the stress experienced depend upon the nature and number of problems, intensity of the problems this area was included as one of the variables in this study.

Family Stress with a Mentally Handicapped Child

1. Constant psychological stress, negative effect on the other siblings, misunderstandings within the family, decreased interaction with the neighbours and relatives, economic loss were significant factors associated with the families of retarded children.
2. Mentally handicapped child's characteristics like temperament, responsiveness, repetitive behavioural patterns and care-giving demands were significantly related to the amount of stress reported by the mothers.
3. Single parents experienced more stress with mentally handicapped children.

4. Familial adaptation to stress with a mentally handicapped child depends on the availability of coping resources.
5. Family stress with a mentally handicapped child was at a higher level at specific transition periods, namely, when the child was entering adolescence and young-adulthood.
6. Child characteristics and family crisis–meeting resources were significant predictors of various forms of stress.
7. Stress management training, if added, in the pool of interventions would be of great help to the parents of mentally handicapped children.
8. Mothers reported more stress from the personal consequences of parenting than fathers, with mentally handicapped children.
9. Stress was negatively associated with informal support, for both parents and positively associated with increased care-giving requirements for mothers.
10. Parents perceived daily stress, the child's low level of functioning and the child's behaviour problems strongly influenced the parent's placement decision in an institution.
11. Parent's perceptions about their mentally handicapped children, their disability, how it is affecting the family, need to be understood by professionals who render services.
12. Parents' stress attributed to care and management of the child with intellectual disability was found to be related to the extent of child's dependence and the extent of child's behaviour problems. Hence, parental perceptions are a vital component to the formulations of family focused interventions.
13. Mother's problem focused coping correlated positively with their children's constructive behaviour and negatively with their children's behaviour disturbance. Father's emotion focused coping was found to be positively and significantly related to their children's school achievement.
14. Mothers of children in the middle childhood group had

higher stress scores than mothers of pre-school and adolescent groups. The middle childhood group reported significantly greater frequency of behaviour problems.

15. Parental burden with a mentally handicapped child in the form of interference in their family routine or leisure and recreation, which resulted in social, marital, familial and emotional problems in the home setting.
16. No significant differences in the perceived burden with reference to the sex of the child were observed.
17. Mothers of mentally handicapped children most commonly resort to the coping styles like denial, rehearsal of outcome, finding a purpose and seeking emotional support.
18. Mothers reported higher social burden with mentally handicapped children. Mothers of female mentally handicapped children perceived more burden in the areas of disruption in family leisure and effect on mental health of the mother. Most of the mothers reported, moderate, to severe burden.
19. The nature and type of perceived burden by family members of mentally handicapped child may range from difficulties in transportation, management of child's behaviour problems, disruption of daily routine, economic, physical and/or social burden.
20. Some families eliminated the stressor (handicapped child) by placing the child out of home.

Stress experienced by the individual or the individual family depend upon how individuals perceive this stress. So, review of relevant studies helped the investigator to include the perception of stressful effects by various individuals in the family as one of the objectives of study. However, it is dependent on how coherent the family is and/or how the family performed its functions.

Influence of Mentally Handicapped Child and Family Functioning

1. Family functioning is affected by the presence of mentally handicapped child. Level of family functioning increased over

an interval of one year for families that institutionalized the child and decreased for those that kept the child at home.

2. Family functioning varied depending on the availability of support systems in families with mentally handicapped child.

3. Marital disharmony, family quarreling were common in these families.

4. Some families respond to the care of a child with resilience and result in adaptive functioning.

5. Behaviour disturbance in mentally handicapped children is common in dysfunctional families.

6. Single parents especially mothers of handicapped children were more dissatisfied with family functioning.

7. The highest rate of behaviour disturbance in children with mental retardation is associated with higher rates of psychiatric disturbance in parents.

8. Although marital satisfaction declined after the birth of a retarded child, their marital satisfaction prior to the birth of this child determined how well they coped with the situation.

9. Marital conflict, strictness with children, easy irritation with children, suppression of aggression and avoidance of communication were some of the trends observed in families with retarded children.

10. Siblings perceptions of mentally handicapped child mostly depend on their parent's perceptions. Parents often offer a model to them as to how to respond to the mentally retarded.

A review of studies on family functioning helped to find out how this dimension is influenced by the components presents in family. After a review of relevant studies in this section family functioning was selected as one of the variables for the present study.

Support Systems to Families with a Mentally Handicapped Child

1. Social networks are very important aids to successful coping

and adaptation for the parents of mentally handicapped child.

2. Social isolation in families with mentally handicapped child is an often reported finding.

3. Neither the severity of the handicap nor tangible support services were significantly related to maternal stress associated with caring for a handicapped child.

4. Actual social support is less important than perceived social support because an individual may under-estimate or over-estimate support resources.

5. Support and help received from extended family members was perceived more valuable than from friends.

6. Parent training programmes need to be intervened to enhance marital satisfaction, increase family adaptability and decrease stress.

Much depends on how the family perceives and receives the various support systems available in the family and community. After reviewing the studies related to effectiveness of supports available, it is decided to include perceptions of members regarding the support systems.

An extensive review of literature made it possible for presentation of some salient observations under classified headings. All these observations were used in the conceptualization of the problem, selection of variables and formation of questions for experimental verification.

3

Statement of the Problem and Hypotheses

Justification

Mental Handicap forms a significant problem affecting the lives of mentally handicapped individuals and their families. The nature of mental handicap is, "arrested or delayed development", which means, that there is both a limited level of functioning, as well as, need for additional supports from the family and community over long periods of life.

There is no doubt, to believe that having a mentally handicapped child in the family, calls for a lot of adjustments on the part of parents and other family members. The impact of such a child on the family may be so great that parents may often require considerable time and help in order to achieve an emotional acceptance of the child and the handicap.

Prevalence of Mental Retardation in India

There has never been a nation-wide survey to understand the magnitude of mental retardation. However, a number of studies have been undertaken in different populations, special groups of people and school children. Studies of school children and child population conducted at Mysore, Bangalore, Chandigarh and Delhi indicate a prevalence rate of 2 per cent of population and those with severe degree would be 3–4/1000 population. Majority of mentally handicapped people are below 15 years of age. Prevalence of mental disability is more in rual areas where the bulk of population live, than in urban areas.

Reasons for Undertaking the Present Investigation

The investigator had been closely associated with some families having mentally handicapped children and with a residential institution (Thakur Hari Prasad Institute of Research and Rehabilitation for the Mentally Handicapped, Hyderabad–THPIRRMH) which is offering services to the mentally handicapped children, for the past one and half decades. So was the genesis of genuine interest in the welfare of mentally handicapped children. Another reason for the interest in this field can be traced to the after effects of the rural screening camp at Chandragiri, Andhra Pradesh in the mother of February, 1989. The camp was conducted by THPIRRMH in collaboration with Bala Sevika Training Institute, Tirupati, for which the present investigator was then working as Principal. Looking at the plight of parents of mentally handicapped children during the camp, the present investigator had an empathetic feeling and wanted to translate her genuine interest into research which may yield some concrete suggestions to parents in coping up with the situation.

The present investigation examines the difficulties and problems faced by the family of a mentally handicapped child in rearing and managing the affairs. Most of the researchers in our country have addressed themselves to find the prevalence and/or certain demographic aspects of mentally handicapped children in the community. The best way to rehabilitate a mentally handicapped child, is to provide help to the family in managing the child within its natural habitat. This applies particularly, to such of those children who have mild and moderate mental handicap. What is intended in the present investigation is to go into details of family resources and other support systems available in managing these children. Particular focus is given to study the coping patterns adapted by the families to overcome the stressful experience of having a mentally handicapped child.

Perceptions of different family members with regard to issues related to rearing and managing mentally handicapped child need to be studied in order to understand the influence of such a child on family functioning. Family members may adapt different coping strategies to handle the problems and difficulties with a mentally handicapped child. Family members' assessment of their satisfaction about how their family is functioning may be helpful in understanding the family conditions of mentally handicapped children.

Behaviour problems are very common with mentally handicapped children. This may cause an additional stress on the presents. This additional stress may be reflected in their role performance as parents, ultimately affecting family functioning.

Hypotheses

The following hypotheses were formulated principally based on the available literature reviewed in the previous chapter.

1. Fathers, mothers and significant other persons differ significantly in their perceptions about stressful effects on the family in rearing and managing a mentally handicapped child.
2. Socio-demographic variables significantly influence the family functioning in families with a metnally handicapped child.
3. Family variables like type and size of the family, family resources and family satisfaction, significantly influence the family functioning in families with a mentally handicapped child.
4. The perceptions of family members about the burden of raising a mentally handicapped child significantly influence the family functioning.
5. Behaviour problems exhibited by the mentally handicapped child significantly influenced the family functioning.
6. The impact of mentally handicaped child on family functioning cannot be predicted with the help of independent variables as perceived by fathers, mothers and significant other persons.

Little is known about the capacities of the families, their

resources and constraints, in providing care for children. The need for family research in this area cannot be over emphasized as many of the mentally handicapped children in Indian population are in the late childhood and adolescence period. A research based on variables, issues concerned with families of mentally handicapped children may throw some light on how these families can be helped by intervention programmes. Research of this nature may help to develop awareness programmes in the community with reference to their nature and use.

Present research is undertaken with a view to know the needs, resources, capabilities and constraints of families in managing the stress of raising a mentally handicapped child. The details of methodology tools and the quantitative procedures employed are described in the next chapter.

4

Methodology

General Plan

The major aim of the study is to understand the stressful effects the family experiences in raising a mentally handicapped child in the light of resources and support systems available to the family. With this purpose the present study is planned to be conducted in two stages. The first stage : pilot study which is meant for preliminary evaluation of major tools and the procedures to be finally employed. The second stage is concerned about the collection of primary data on a selected sample of families with mentally handicapped children according to the standard procedure and design of the study.

A sample of sixty (60) families with mentally handicapped children from Chandragiri Mandal in Chittoor District (Andhra Pradesh) was selected. The sample selection was made using purposive sampling technique. The sample selection was based on a rural screening camp conducted by Thakur Hari Prasad Institute of Research and Rehabilitation for the Mentally Handicapped in collaboration with Bala Sevika Training Institute (Tirupati) for which the present investigator was then working as Principal. One hundred and forty six (146) children were identified as mentally handicapped and out of them only one hundred and seventeen (117) children attended the screening camp (Report by THPI). A sample of seventy (70) children were selected for both pilot and finally study (10 for pilot study and 60 for final study) whose families were the main focus of the study.

Brief Profile of the Area

A brief picture of the living conditions and life styles of the people in the rural area covered by the camp is relevant at this juncture. Description is limited to those aspects which have direct relevance to the tackling of the problem of mental handicap.

Majority of the people are illiterate and the literate population that constitute 18 per cent is dominated by men. The educational level of the literate heads of the family ranged from standard I to VII. The main occupation of the people of the area is agricultural labour, petty business and cattle rearing. These occupations are seasonal and most of the people are daily wage earners with no steady income. The living conditions are also not very hygienic and the homes are crammed and congested. Unhealthy practices like early marriages are still very common in these areas leading to very early conception and closely spaced children which are high risk factors for disability among children. Consanguineous marriages were also commonly found.

The variables were defined based on the research information available for further probe. In addition to age, gender, birth order and social class, family variables like type of marriage, type of family, number of family members, family integration, family coping, family burden and family satisfaction and the dependent variable family functioning were also included.

In the first stage of the study the tools were evaluated for their suitability for the measurement of various variables concerned. In the second stage data on both dependent and independent variables were obtained on a sample of families with mentally handicapped children.

Subjects for Preliminary Study

Ten (10) families with a mentally handicapped child were selected. Both the parents of the handicapped child and a significant other person were the respondents. Among families of those mentally handicapped children who participated in the screening camp children belonging to childhood, late childhood and adolescent age groups were chosen (10 × 3 = 30).

Final Study

Sixty (60) families having mentally handicapped children constituted the sample. Mentally handicapped children belonging to three age groups namely childhood, late childhood and adolescence were chosen for the final study.

Tools and Materials of Research

The following tools were used in data collection.

1. Socio-Economics Status Scale (Rural) (Trivedi and Uday Pareek, 1964)
2. Family Resources Scale (FRS) (Developed by the Investigator)
3. Family coping Scale (FCS) (Developed by the Investigator)
4. Family Functioning Scale (FFS) (Developed by the Investigator)
5. Family Integration Scale (FIS) (Developed by the Investigator)
6. Family Burden Scale (FBS) (Pai and Kapur, 1981)
7. Family Satisfaction Scale (FSS) (Smilkstein, 1978)
8. Problem Behaviour Checklist (PBCL) (Peshawaria et al., 1990)

Description of the Tools

1. Socio-Economic Status Scale

The Socio-Economic Status Scale (Rural) developed by Trivedi and Pareek (1964) was chosen as it was thought suitable for rural area. This tool consisted of nine items where in all details about caste, occupation, education, social participation, land, house, farm-power, material possessions and family were included.

These nine items were found to be significant in indicating the socio-economic status of a rural family. The items included in the scale are such that, information can be easily collected about these.

The scale has the added advantage in its simplicity of administration. Items are such that, the scale facilitates collection of quantitative and objective information. Thus little subjective judgment of the investigator is involved in the collection of the data.

The items on the scale are related both to the head of the family and the family itself. The first seven items are of graded scale type. This means that each item is scaled from the lowest to the highest, each sub-item representing a point on the scale. This also means that only one of the sub-items is to be checked for a particular respondent under each of the first seven items.

On the other hand items 8 and 9 are additive in nature. In item 8 all the five sub-items are to be checked and scored. In items 9 either of the sub-items in both (a) and (b) has to be checked in addition to (c)–total checks being three.

Procedure for Administration

The information needed for checking on the scale was collected by simple interview. After collecting information on the items the total score was calculated. Depending upon the total score obtained by the family, the family can be categorized under A, B, C, D and E groups.

Rationale

The criteria on scores used for classification of the different categories are given below:

Symbol	Category	Scores on the Scale
A	Upper Class	Above 43
B	Upper Middle Class	33–42
C	Middle Class	24–32
D	Lower Middle Class	13–23
E	Lower Class	Below 13

2. Family Resources Scale (F.R.S.)

Description

This scale was specially devised for the purpose of the present investigation by the investigator. The scale covered ten different items like community resources for health, education and recreational facilities, respondent's health, respondent's problem solving skills, positive beliefs, marital issues, extended family issues, information related to close friends, neighbours and membership in professional and social service agencies. The responses were rated on a three point rating scale.

Ex : Health of the Respondents

Not so Good	Good	Very Good
1	2	3

1. How was your health before the birth of this child ?
2. How is your health at present ?

Scoring

If the response was 'not so good' a score of 1 was given, for response 'very good' a score of 3 was given.

Ten different areas covered fifty six questions. So the score ranged from 56–168.

Administration

After establishing initial rapport the items were read out and the responses were recorded on a three point rating scale.

Rationale

Greater the score the higher are the family resources.

3. Family Coping Scale

Description of the Tool

This scale was developed by the investigator to assess the coping skills of family members with a mentally handicapped child. This consists of twelve (12) questions related to various styles of coping. The responses were rated on a three point rating scale. Among the twelve questions, half of them indicate negative coping and half indicate positive coping. Following is an example for positive coping style. "Do you want to discuss your problems with other parents having retarded children" ?

Never	Sometimes	Always
1	2	3

An example for negative coping style is as follows. "Do you consider that it happened because of your past sins?"

Never	Sometimes	Always
3	2	1

For positive coping style a score of '1' is given to the response "Never" '2' is given to the response "sometimes" and '3' is given to the response "always", whereas for negative coping style the scoring order is just reversed. The expected minimum score is 12 and the maximum being 36.

Rationale

Higher score indicates greater and better coping skills.

4. Family Functioning Scale

Family functioning scale was developed by the investigator as a four point rating scale. Families vary in the number of functions on which they focus as well as in the degree to which they perform any particular function. Families also differ in terms of how and whether they seek and obtain help from services agencies, friends, extended family members and others. This scale assesses the impact of a mentally handicapped child on family functioning.

Administration

After establishing initial rapport the schedule was presented to the respondents to collect information on the overall picture of family functioning. The scale has fifty statements under nine different family functions. They are;

1. Physical care function
2. Rest and recuperation
3. Economic function
4. Affectional function

5. Educational function
6. Guidance function
7. Vocational function
8. Socialisation function, and
9. Self-definition function

Scoring

Each statement has four categories of responses. "Not at all" response gets a score of '1' "Mildly" response gets a score of 2, "Moderately"–3, "Severely"–4. Possible minimum score is fifty (50) and possible maximum score is two hundred (200).

Rationale

All answers from first category indicate no effect on family functioning. Middle two responses indicate in between intensities. Responses of fourth category indicate extreme effect on family functioning. Higher the score, severe is the effect on family functioning.

5. Family Integration Scale

Measures the cohesion and adaptability thereby gives us an indication whether the family is an integrated one or disintegrated. It consisted of twelve questions with dichotomized answers (Yes/No).

Scoring

All 'Yes' responses are taken into consideration. 'No' responses are left out. 1 score is given to each 'Yes' response. The total number of 'Yes' responses indicate the level of family integration present in that particular family. The score ranged from 0–12 indicating the level of integration present in the family.

Rationale

A higher score indicates greater integration whereas a lower score indicates poor integration.

6. Family Burden Scale

Family Burden Scale developed by Pai and Kapur (1981) was

used to assess the burden felt by the family members with a mentally handicapped child. According to Pai and Kapur family burden denotes the dysfunction in some of the important functioning pattern due to the chronic Schizophrenia.

The interview schedule concentrates on six areas namely;

1. Financial burden.
2. Disruption of family routine activities.
3. Disruption of family leisure.
4. Disruption of family interaction.
5. Effect on physical health of others.
6. Effect on mental health of others and subjective burden.

Scoring

Each and every item was scored on a three point scale i.e., score '2' was given for the response "Severe", Score '1' for "Moderate" response and '0' for nil or no burden. Possible score ranges from '0' Indicating no burden to '50' indicating severe burden.

Rationale

Higher score indicates greater level of burden and vice-versa.

7. Family Satisfaction Scale

This was developed by Smilkstein (1978) which is a short self administered questionnaire. There is evidence that this instrument format is relatively easy to administer and has reasonable reliability as well as face and criterion validity. Another advantage is the family member's ratings are used rather than expert's assessment.

There is consensus among psychometricians that a 5 point continuum–elicits a more valid distribution of response and improves reliability (Wore et al., 1976).

Family Satisfaction Scale has nine (9) statements for which the responses are rated on a 5 point rating scale. The responses indicate the level of satisfaction with various essential expressive activities ' the family.

Scoring

The respondents are asked to respond to statements about the family by checking one of the five responses after each statement.

Not at all	1
Not very	2
More or less	3
Quite a lot	4
Very much	5

The score ranges from a minimum of 9 to a maximum of 45.

Rationale

A greater score indicates higher family satisfaction.

8. Problem Behaviour Check List

This was developed by Peshawaria et al., (1990) at NIMH. This check-list consisted of behaviour problems classified under twelve categories namely :

1. Physical harm towards others
2. Damages property
3. Misbehaves with others
4. Temper tantrums
5. Wanders
6. Disobedience
7. Repetitive Behaviour
8. Self-injurious behaviour
9. Restless and physically overactive
10. Odd behaviour
11. Fears
12. Sexual problems

Scoring

Each problem reported was given 1 score and added up total score gives the number of problems manifested in the child's behaviour.

Rationale

Higher the score greater are the behaviour problems reported by respondents.

Here one fact must be remembered. Many studies on families with mentally handicapped members have been criticized because of lack of non-handicapped comparison groups. In classic experimental designs control groups are used to reduce the number of potential alternate explanations for a given effect. The aim here is to hold all factors constant except the variables under study. This type of control can never be achieved in family research.

Baummister (1984) questioned the rationale for the large number of comparison group studies in mental retardation research and described comparison studies as an unnecessary excursion into a theoretical swamp inhabited by all sorts of conceptual and methodological monsters. Although comparison studies have much to contribute, comparison groups are not a necessity in family research. With regard to tools and instruments used in comparative research, it may not be appropriate to use the same instruments with control and experimental groups. Numerous investigators (Dyson and Fewell, 1986; Friedrich and Friedrich, 1981; Salisbury, 1987; Wilton and Renaut, 1986) have used the original and revised version of Questionnaire on Resources and Stress to ascertain whether families with mentally retarded children experienced more stress than do comparison families. Because this scale was designed for families coping with a mentally handicapped child, numerous items have little or no possibility of occurrence among comparison families.

It is against these methodological clarification it was decided to study the stressful effects experienced by family with a mentally handicapped child.

Procedure for Initial Study

Ten (10) families were selected from a group of families which were identified to be having a mentally handicapped child at the rural screening camp in the year 1989. The procedure adopted was purposive sampling or judgment sampling as the aim of the investigation was to study the stressful effects and coping styles of families in raising a mentally handicapped child. Those families satisfying the following conditions were included in the sample.

1. Only those families which had mentally handicapped children whose age ranged from 6–18 years along were selected.
2. Both the parents must be living together with the child.
3. Those families where the mentally handicapped child had an elder brother, sister, grand-father/grand-mother, aunt/uncle or any other significant person living in the same family or closeby.
4. Only those families which attended the camp were taken as population.

Both the parents and one significant other person were interviewed separately following the standard procedure and their responses were recorded. Interview session was split into two halves, each half lasting about 30–40 minutes. In the first session family resources scale, and family functioning scale were administered and in the second session, coping scale, family burden scale, family integration scale, family satisfaction scale, and problem behaviour check-list were administered.

The data thus collected on each tool was examined for the suitability in terms of language difficulty and appropriateness. Wherever necessary the terms were changed by substituting better items or rewording for clarity. Items found unsuitable were omitted.

The pilot study has not only helped to find out the suitability of tools but also created an awareness about the problems to be encountered in collecting qualitative and quantitative data in a rural setting. Further the experience was found extremely useful in employing better methods of interviewing and handling the situation. Especially the experience helped the investigator to learn better problem solving techniques in handling parents of mentally handicapped children. The efficacy of the tools developed for the present research were examined. In order to see whether all the items of the scales were sufficiently reliable, the percentage of respondents in the sample attempting to answer a given item in the expected manner was calculated. In such analysis, items which were answered by a large number of respondents were retained and the items which were answered by fewer number of respondents were eliminated.

Another way of evaluating the efficacy is by calculating their reliability. Split-half reliability coefficients were calculated for the four tools developed.

Table 4.1 : Split-half Reliability Values for the Tools Developed

S. No.	*Description of the Tool*	*Split-half reliability*
1.	Family Resources Scale (FRS)	0.66
2.	Family Coping Scale (FCS)	0.64
3.	Family Functioning Scale (FFS)	0.81
4.	Family Integration Scale (FIS)	0.64

Procedure for Final Study

The procedure employed for selection of sample for final study was identical to the procedure of sample selection for initial study. Using purposive sampling technique sixty (60) families fulfilling the requirements of age of the child, presence of both in-living parents and presence of a significant other person were selected from the population of families with mentally handicapped children who were identified in the rural screening camp. However, the subjects in the final study were totally new that is to say, that none of the families in the initial study were allowed into final sample.

Procedure for Collection of Data

The major tools described earlier were administered to both the parents of each child, and a significant other person independently. Different tools were administered in two sessions as in the initial study. The data thus collected was scored, means and SDS were calculated and then subjected to suitable statistical techniques as described below :

The data were carefully analysed and appropriate statistical techniques like 't' test 'F' ration were employed to know whether the independent variables could influence significantly the dependent variable.

The correlation coefficient (r) was computed between each one of the independent variables and dependent variable viz., family functioning to identify the most significant variables associated with dependent variable. The multiple correlation coefficient 'R' was calculated by carrying out the step-wise regression analysis to find out the differential contribution of socio-economic, demographic variables and family variables in predicting dependent variable. 't' test, 'F' ratio, correlation coefficient (r), multiple correlation coefficient (R) and multiple regression were calculated by employing the usual procedures (Garrett, 1979; Kothari, 1986). Analysis and interpretation of data are dealt in detail in the next chapter.

Analysis and Interpretation of Data

This chapter deals with the statistical analysis of the data collected and interpretation of the results against existing theoretical background. The results are presented in five sections.

Section-I	Characteristics and Composition of the Sample
Section-II	Descriptive Analysis
Section-III	Inter-group differences
Section-IV	Correlational Analysis
Section-V	Step-wise Multiple Regression Analysis

Section-I
Characteristics and Composition of the Sample

i) Mentally Handicapped Children (MHC)

A sample of sixty children identified as mentally handicapped in the screening camp and whose ages ranged from 6 to 18 years were included. These children were classified into three groups depending upon their chronological age; children from 6 to 10 years are in the "childhood" group; 11 to 14 years are in the "late childhood" group; and 15 to 18 years are in the "adolescence" group (Table 5.1).

Table 5.1 : Classification of MHC according to Age

S. No.	*Group*	*Age Group*	*Number*	*Percent-age*
1.	Childhood	6–10	21	35.0
2.	Late childhood	11–14	22	36.7
3.	Adolescence	15–18	17	28.3
	Total		60	100.0

Around 35 per cent of the children in the sample belonged to the two childhood groups each and the remaining (28.3%) children belonged to the adolescent group.

Majority (65%) of the children in the sample are boys and maximum number of children (45%) are the first born and all the others put together constitute fifty five per cent (55%) of the sample (Table 5.2).

Table 5.2 : Classification of MHC according to Gender and Ordinal Position

Category	*Group*	*Number*	*Percentage*
Gender	Female	21	35
	Male	39	65
Ordinal Position	First born	27	45
	Later born	33	55

ii) Respondents for the Study

Father, mother and significant other person in the family of each of the sixty children were the respondents. So altogether there were one hundred and eighty (180) respondents. (60 fathers, 60 mothers and 60 significant other persons). Their distribution on the basis of their age and type of marriage is described in Table 5.3.

Around seventy one (71.6) per cent of the marriages of parents were consanguineous and the remaining 28.4 per cent were

Table 5.3 : Classification of Respondents According to Age

Respondents	*Age Range (Years)*	*Number*	*Percentage*
Fathers	30–45	32	53.4
	46–65	28	46.6
Mothers	25–40	35	58.4
	41–65	25	41.6
Significant Other Persons	17–40	33	55.0
	41–75	27	45.0

non-consanguineous.

iii) Characteristics of Families of the Respondents

Ninety (90) per cent of the families belonged to Hindu religion and the remaining ten (10) per cent were Muslims. There were no Christians in the sample.

With regard to the structure of the family nearly half of (48.3%) the families belonged to nuclear type and one third (33.4%) of the families are of joint type and the remaining (18.3%) are extended type. Majority of the families (67%) had one to three children and one third (33%) of the families had four and more than four children.

Around fifty seven (56.6) per cent of the families were small in size where the number of family members ranged from three to six. Remaining forty three (43.4) per cent families were large in size wherein the number of family members were seven and more than seven (Table 5.4).

The composition of family members under the third category namely "significant other person" is shown in Table 5.5.

Different members considered as "significant other persons" were classified into five categories depending upon the relationship of that person to the target child. These five categories were grouped together in two different ways for the sake of analysis. The first grouping is based on the relationships irrespective of the fact that they are from maternal side or paternal side. Grand parents irrespective of the fact whether they are paternal or maternal are

Table 5.4 : Classification of Families according to Structure, Number of Children and Number of Family Members

S.No.	Family Variables	Number	Percentage
1.	STRUCTURE OF FAMILY		
	Nuclear	29	48.3
	Extended	11	18.3
	Joint	20	33.4
2.	NUMBER OF CHILDREN		
	1–3 Children	37	67.0
	4 and above	23	33.0
3.	NUMBER OF FAMILY MEMBERS		
	Small (3–6)	34	56.6
	Large (7 and above)	26	43.4

Table 5.5 : Classification of Distribution of Significant Other Persons'

S.No.	Description of Relationship	Number	Percentage
1.	Grand Parents	27	45.00
2.	Aunts and Uncles	14	23.33
3.	Siblings	19	31.67
	Total	60	100.00

considered as one group. This category consisted of 27 members. Aunts and uncles from both paternal and maternal side were considered as the second group with 14 members. Out of sixty the remaining 19 were the siblings of the target child.

Another classification considered for analysis is a little different as shown in Table 5.6. Siblings (n=19) as one group, paternal side relatives (n=31) as the second group and maternal side relatives (n=10) as the third group.

The mean scores presented in Table 5.7 show that the three groups of respondents viz. fathers', mothers' and SOPs' scored in a similar manner. As the classification given by the authors with regard to SES scale as described in Chapter-4 almost all the respondents had just crossed the lower middle class bracket (13–23). However the mean scores indicate that all the respondents are in

Table 5.6 : Second Classification of Significant Other Persons

S.No.	*Description*	*Number*	*Percentage*
1.	Siblings	19	31.67
2.	Paternal side relatives	31	51.67
3.	Maternal side relatives	10	16.66
	Total	60	100.00

Table 5.7 : Mean Scores obtained by Fathers, Mothers and SOPs on Eight Scales used for Collection of Data

S.No.	*Scale*	*Fathers* mean N=60		*Mothers* Mean N=60		SOPs Mean N=60	
		$\overline{X}$	(SD)	$\overline{X}$	(SD)	$\overline{X}$	(SD)
1.	SES	25.06	(5.058)	23.28	(4.759)	24.50	(4.560)
2.	FRS	85.65	(3.982)	84.85	(3.282)	84.10	(4.144)
3.	FCS	21.33	(1.590)	20.60	(1.509)	21.68	(1.845)
4.	FIS	7.78	(1.222)	7.78	(1.341)	7.98	(1.241)
5.	FBS	20.08	(4.570)	19.65	(3.820)	18.56	(4.330)
6.	FFS	143.50	(18.277)	145.23	(17.552)	143.86	(16.173)
7.	FSS	25.21	(3.405)	24.53	(4.094)	25.60	(9.295)
8.	BP	3.85	(0.917)	3.83	(0.866)	3.88	(0.922)

the middle class. (Fathers' mean 25.06, mothers' mean 23.28 and SOPs mean 24.50).

The mean scores obtained by the three groups of respondents on Family Resources Scale (FRS) are 85.65, 84.85 and 84.10 respectively. The possible minimum score on this scale is 56.00 and the possible maximum score is 168.00. The mid point being 112.00 the mean scores of the three groups of respondents are below the mid point.

Even on Family Coping Scale (FCS) the three groups did not cross the mid point in their mean scores. (Mid point is 24.00). The obtained mean scores by fathers, mothers and SOPs are 21.33,

20.60 and 21.68 respectively.

The mean scores on Family Integration Scale (FIS) obtained by the three groups of respondents is the same. (X_1 = 7.78, X_2 = 7.78 and X_3 = 7.98). The mid point being 6.00 all the three groups of respondents scored above the mid point.

The Family Burden Scale assessed (FBS) the burden felt by the three groups with a Mentally Handicapped Child (MHC) in their family. The mid point on this scale is 25.00 and the obtained mean scores are 20.08, 19.68 and 18.56 respectively indicating that all the three groups scored less than the midpoint. It may be inferred that three groups of respondents perceived a little less than "moderate burden" (as per the classification given by Pai and Kapur 1981). But there is a little variation in the mean scores obtained by the three groups of respondents. Fathers scored a higher mean score than the other groups. Significant other persons did not feel the burden as much as the other two groups felt.

The mean scores on Family Functioning Scale (FFS) as obtained by the three groups of respondents did not vary much. The mid point is 125 and all the three groups of respondents perceived the impact of mentally handicapped child on family functioning approximately upto 75%.

With regard to family satisfaction (FS) the midpoint is 27.0. All the three groups scored a mean just a little less than the mid point. (25.21, 24.53 and 25.60 respectively).

As far as behaviour problems are concerned all the three groups perceived 33% of behaviour problems in their MHC. The maximum score being 12.00 and the mean scores obtained by the three groups is approximately 4. However the means computed for the three groups of respondents on all eight scales fail to explain the groups differences in a meaningful manner. So further analysis was planned to measure the differences in perceptions of the three groups of respondents.

As a next step in the analysis, the classifications described in the first section viz., Classification of children according to their age, gender, ordinal position, classification of respondents according to age and type of marriage, and classification of families according to type, number of children and size were made use of to see the significant differences in the perceptions of three groups of respondents on all scales. Preliminary analysis using the above classification did not yield significant differences among the groups, which indicate that these variables viz., child's age, gender and ordinal position did not affect the perceptions of the three groups of respondents. Respondents age and the type of their marriage also did not exert any influence on their perceptions.

Among the family variables, type of family could only influence the perceptions of significant other persons whereas, family size exerted its influence on both fathers'and mothers'perceptions only on two scales. Hence the classifications described in the I section were not utilized for further analysis. The respondents were considered as three independent groups as fathers, mothers and SOPs from hereafter.

Section–II
Descriptive Analysis

The family functioning scale has 50 items covering all the nine family functions. The items are ranked on a four point rating scale as described in Chapter 4. Minimum possible score is 50 and maximum possible score is 200. The total score on these 50 items described the impact of MHC on family functioning as perceived by fathers, mothers and significant other persons.

Father's Perceptions

The mean, median and mode obtained by fathers are 143.50, 149.00 and 160.00 respectively. The scores obtained by fathers ranged from 95 to 171. Theoretically the score ranges from 50–200. Since the obtained mean is higher than half of the theoretically possible score, i.e., 100 (200/2 = 100). It can be concluded that the fathers in general perceived a great impact of MHC on family functioning.

The frequency distribution Table 5.8 clearly indicates that almost all fathers scored above 100 except one. The skewness and Kurtosis of the distribution are found to be –0.106 and 0.256 respectively. The values indicate that there is negative skewness in distribution and it is leptokurtic as shown in Fig. 5.1. The Standard Deviation (SD) of the distribution is 18.1241 with 95 as the

Table 5.8 : Frequency Distribution Scores on the Impact of MHC on FF as Perceived by Fathers

Class Interval	*Frequencies*	*Cumulative Frequencies*	*Smoothed Frequencies*
95–106	2	2	2.66
107–118	6	8	4.66
119–130	6	14	6.00
131–142	6	20	11.66
143–154	23	43	14.66
155–166	15	58	13.33
167–178	2	60	5.66

minimum score and 171 as the maximum score. The range is 76 and Quartile Deviation (QD) of the distribution is 12.50.

Mother's Perceptions

The mean, median and mode are 145.23, 151.00 and 162.53 respectively. The score obtained by mothers ranged from 101 to 168. Almost all mothers secured higher score than half of the possible theoretical score. It can be understood that the mother's perception of the impact of MHC on family functioning is great. The skewness and Kurtosis are –0.994 and 0.214 respectively. The values indicate that there is negative skewness in the distribution and it is slightly leptokurtic (Fig. 5.2). The Standard Deviation (SD) is 17.4053. The range is 67 and the Quartile Deviation of the distribution is 8.50.

Table 5.9 : Frequency Distribution Scores on the Impact of MHC on FF as Perceived by Mothers

Class Interval	*Frequencies*	*Cumulative Frequencies*	*Smoothed Frequencies*
100–114	5	5	4.00
115–129	7	12	7.00
130–144	9	21	14.33
145–159	27	48	16.00
160–174	12	60	13.00

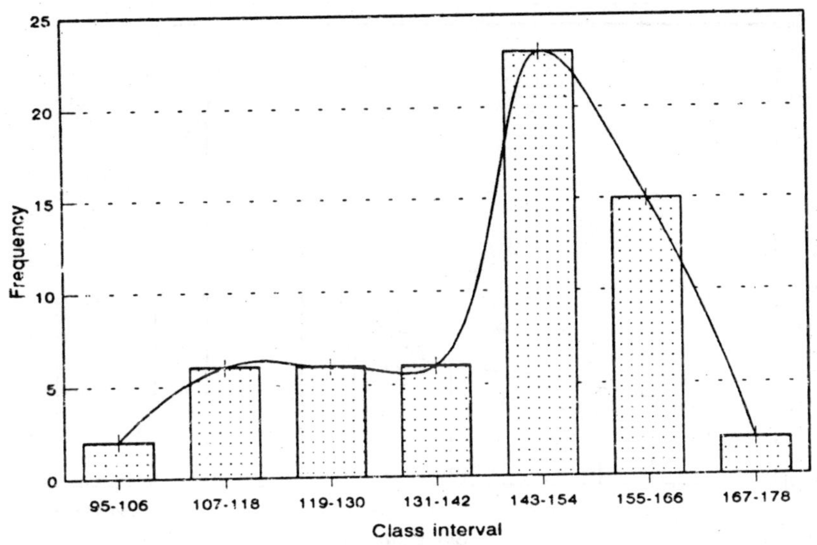

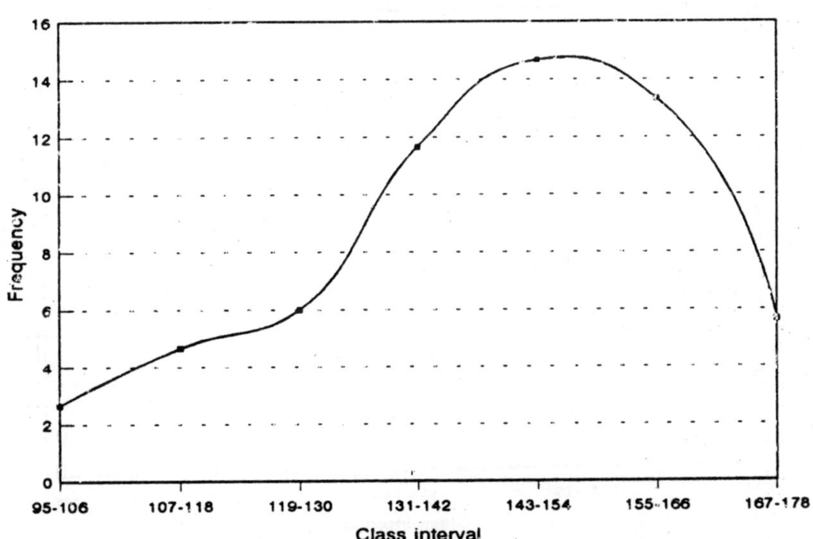

Fig. 5.1 : Distribution of Scores on the Impact of MHC on FF as Perceived by Fathers

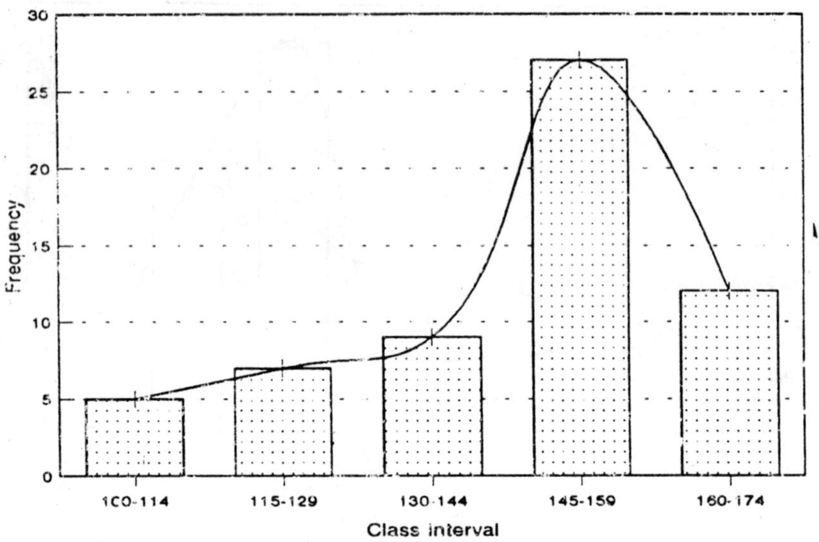

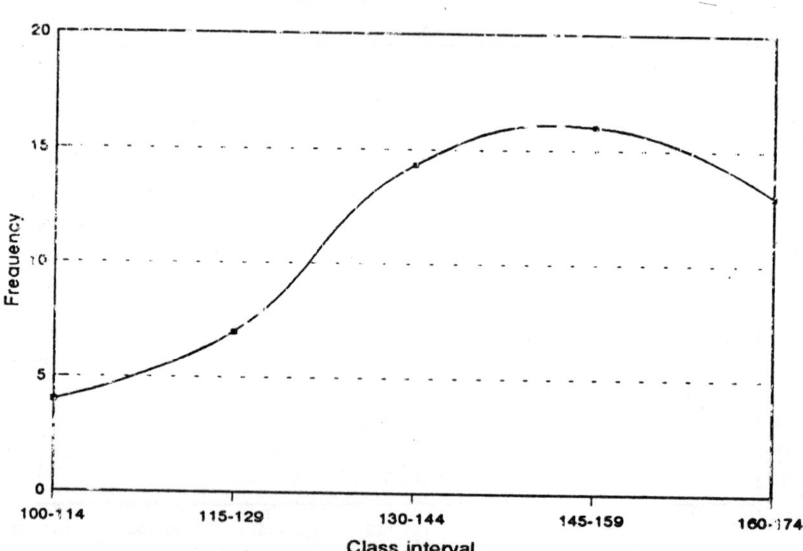

Fig. 5.2 : Distribution of Scores on the Impact of MHC on FF as Perceived by Mothers

SOPs Perceptions

The mean, median and mode are 143.86, 149.00 and 159.26 respectively. The scores obtained by significant other persons ranged from 100 to 172. The skewness and Kurtosis are –0.961 and 0.188 respectively. The Standard Deviation of the distribution is 16.04 and Quartile Deviation of the distribution is 8.50. The values indicate that there is negative skewness in the distribution and it is slightly leptokurtic (Fig. 5.3).

Table 5.10 : Frequency Distribution Scores on the Impact of MHC on FF as Perceived by Significant Other Persons

Class Interval	*Frequencies*	*Cumulative Frequencies*	*Smoothed Frequencies*
100–114	5	5	4.00
115–129	7	12	7.66
130–144	11	23	16.00
145–159	30	53	16.00
160–174	7	60	7.00

Section–III
Inter-group Differences in Perceptions

An attempt is made to see whether there is any significant difference in the perceptions of three different groups of respondents namely fathers, mothers and significant other persons on various factors. After examining the means, ANOVA was employed to find out to what extent the three groups differ significantly in their perceptions about different aspects of family. The means, SDs and F values are presented in Table 5.11.

Community resources available as per the perceptions of the three categories of respondents were one and the same and did not vary significantly (F = 0.0067) Table 5.11). The area of study being a village, the availability of resources especially community based are meager. Even those meagerly available resources are not within the preview of the respondents as sometimes they are not aware of the existence of the same.

Next in order is perceptions about respondent's health "F"

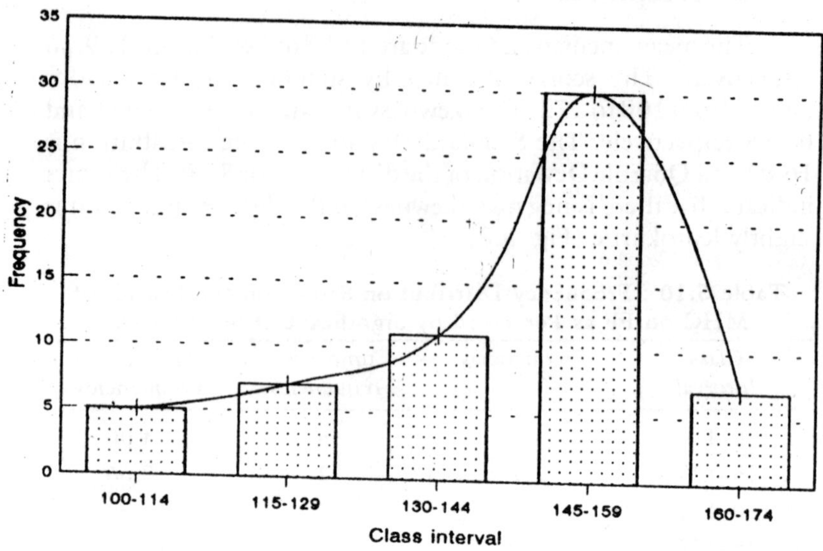

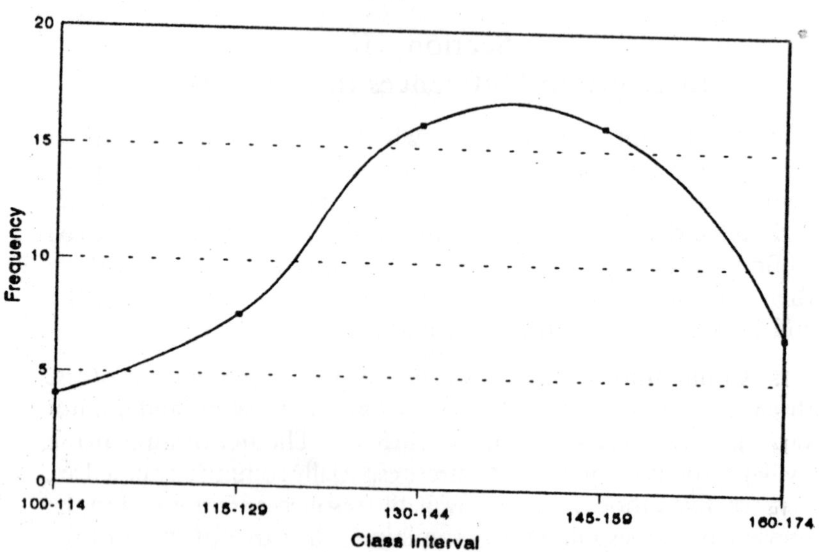

Fig. 5.3 : Distribution of Scores on the Impact of MHC on FF as Perceived by SOPs

Table 5.11 : Means and SDs of Family Resources Scores as Perceived by the Respondents of Those Families with MHC

S.No.	Variable	Father n=60 M (σ)	Mother n=60 M (σ)	SOPs n=60 M (σ)	F
1.	Community Resources	4.60 (1.575)	4.58 (1.654)	4.61 (1.584)	0.0067†
2.	Personal Health	5.81 (0.624)	4.51 (0.9112)	5.71 (0.845)	48.6888**
3.	Problem Solving Skills	4.56 (0.945)	4.36 (0.843)	4.06 (0.989)	4.4134*
4.	Positive Beliefs	12.66 (1.410)	12.75 (1.536)	12.56 (1.240)	0.2578†
5.	Marital Issues	9.95 (0.7231)	10.11 (1.0750)	9.06 (1.655)	12.9689**
6.	Extended Family Support	15.71 (1.530)	16.30 (1.381)	15.33 (1.310)	7.1464**
7.	Close Friends	10.35 (1.400)	10.45 (1.534)	10.70 (1.417)	0.9252†
8.	Neighbours	10.75 (1.098)	10.75 (0.950)	10.75 (0.856)	0.0000†
9.	Social Interactions	4.16 (0.762)	4.00 (0.000)	4.28 (0.975)	2.3791†
10.	Family Resources	85.65 (3.982)	84.85 (3.282)	84.10 (4.144)	2.4652†
11.	Personal Resources	23.05 (1.899)	21.63 (1.982)	22.35 (1.830)	8.2946**
12.	Social Resources	36.86 (3.137)	36.78 (2.623)	37.35 (2.821)	0.6835†
13.	Marital Resources	25.66 (1.590)	26.41 (1.225)	24.40 (2.323)	19.8357**
14.	Material Status	10.66 (5.287)	10.50 (5.147)	10.75 (5.160)	0.3600†
15.	Non-material Status	14.40 (4.830)	12.78 (4.372)	13.75 (3.960)	2.0490†

Note : † indicates not significant
* indicates significant at 0.05 level of probability
** indicates significant at 0.01 level of probability

value from Table 5.11 shows that there is significant difference in their perceptions about their own health status (F = 48.6888**) where in fathers feel more positive about their health status followed by significant other persons and mothers ($\overline{X}_1$ = 5.81, $\overline{X}_2$ = 5.71 and $\overline{X}_3$ = 4.51) respectively. The reason is evident. Mothers frequently express that they are not maintaining good health, because of excessive household work especially in the rural background. The presence of mentally handicapped child may further augment the stress and cause more strain on the health of the mother. The following research evidence support the results of present study in this aspect.

Krauss (1993) reported revealing differences between fathers and mothers with respect to specific dimensions of parenting stress. Mothers reported more difficulty than did fathers in adjusting to personal aspects of parenting and parenthood like parental health and restrictions in role relations with the spouse. MHC needed constant care and supervision and in eighty per cent (80%) of the cases parent's sleep was disturbed (Dupont, 1986).

The greater responsibility that mothers bear for the care of MHC also ensures that the burden of caring for such a child is more likely to affect mother's sense of well being and control (Goldberg et al. 1986).

Problem solving skills are yet another important component of resources. How the individual manages a critical situation depends on one's own problem solving skills. "F" value from Table 5.11 shows that fathers possess, significantly higher level of problem solving skills than the other two groups of respondents. It is evident that in a patriarchal society father figure is the symbol of authority. All major decisions and problems are settled by the father. Hence fathers develop problem solving skills of higher level compared to the other two groups of respondents. ($\overline{X}_1$ = 4.56; $\overline{X}_2$ = 4.36 and $\overline{X}_3$ = 4.06 respectively).

Beliefs especially positive ones have an impact on the individual's behaviour. Very little difference is observed in the mean scores regarding the positive beliefs possessed by the individuals. ($\overline{X}_1$ = 12.66; $\overline{X}_2$ = 12.75 and $\overline{X}_3$ = 12.56). However, an examination of mean values indicate that mothers possess slightly higher level of positive beliefs compared to the fathers and significant other persons. However, the calculated 'F'value fails to reach atleast 0.05 level of significance.

Perceptions of marital issues like marital satisfaction, understanding of family roles, skills involved in consultation and compromise, communicative skills and emotional support rendered to the spouse were analysed according to the three groups of respondents. Results indicate that there is a high significant difference in the perceptions about marital issues (F = 12.9689**). Mothers scored higher mean (10.11) when compared with fathers (9.95) and significant other persons (9.06) regarding marital issues. It is self explanatory as women are expected to show higher level of adjustibility and view everything from a positive perspective.

Extended family support is really a wonderful resource especially for families with mentally handicapped child. Results show that there is a significant difference in the perceptions of three groups of respondents (F = 7.1464). Here again, mothers perceive maximum extent of support from extended family than the other two groups. The reason may be that it is the mother who is in constant close contact with extended family than father and significant other person. Sometimes the mother may also act as spokesperson for her family to be represented in the extended family gatherings.

However, perceptions of fathers, mothers and significant other persons are not significantly differing on availability of help from close friends and neighbours. (F = 0.9252 and 0.0000 respectively). The possible explanation for this may be that in rural areas presence of a mentally handicapped child adds social stigma which bars friends and neighbours from making close contacts with these families.

The three groups of respondents do not significantly differ in their perceptions with regard to social interactions. However the third groups namely significant other persons scored higher mean than the other two groups of respondents.

On the whole the perceptions of fathers, mothers and significant other persons do not differ significantly when all the resources are added (F=2.4652). However a slight difference is observed in the mean scores of three groups of respondents, where in fathers scored higher than the other two groups ($\overline{X}_1 = 85.65$; $\overline{X}_2 = 84.85$;

$\overline{X}_3$ = 84.10). This is an indication that it is the father who pools the resources and dictates the allotment and usage, for the family in the patriarchal setup. For the sake of further analysis the nine components of family resources were grouped into three types of resources namely; 1) Personal resources; 2) Social resources and 3) Marital resources.

Personal health, problem solving skills, and positive beliefs were clubbed under personal resources.

Social resources include community facilities, close friends, neighbours and social interactions.

Marital issues and extended family support were considered as marital resources.

It is also attempted to see whether the groups of respondents differ significantly in their perceptions with regard to these three types of resources namely personal, social and marital resources. ANOVA was employed for this purpose.

The three groups of respondents had similar perceptions with regard to social resources (F=0.6835) but significant difference was observed in the perceptions of three groups of respondents with regard to personal resources as F value was 8.2946. Fathers mean score was 23.05 followed by significant other persons whit a mean score of 22.35 whereas mothers scored very low with a mean score of 21.63.

The next variable is marital resources. The perceptions of the three groups of respondents were subjected to ANOVA. F value, 19.835 was significant at 0.01 level. Mothers secured a high score in the perception of marital resources whereas significant other persons secured a low score. It is interesting to note that mothers secured a lowest score in the perception of personal resources and highest score in the perception of marital resources. Women usually play integrative roles in the Indian family set-up by utilizing the available familial resources, whereas men play instrumental roles utilizing their personal resources. This might be the reason for the significant difference between fathers and mothers.

The components of SES were clubbed together depending upon their similarity and were computed as two different variables they are a) material and b) non-material status. Material status included land, house, farm power and material possessions. Non-material status included caste, occupation, education, social participation, family type and family size.

Lastly the three groups of respondents did not differ significantly in their perceptions about material status and non-material status. But a close observation of mean values of non-material status scores indicate that mothers scored comparatively low than the other two groups. This might be due to the inclusion of items like education and social participation where rural women have a deficit.

The next variable considered for analysis is family burden as perceived by the three groups of respondents owing to the presence of MHC.

Fathers, mothers and significant other persons do not significantly differ in their perceptions in all dimensions of family burden scale. Table 5.12). Fathers perception of burden resulting in

Table 5.12 : Means and SDs of Family Burden Scores as Perceived by the Respondents of Those Families with MHC

S.No.	Variable	Father n=60 M (σ)	Mother n=60 M (σ)	SOPs n=60 M (σ)	F
1.	Financial Burden	6.35 (1.876)	5.83 (1.879)	5.66 (2.039)	2.0380†
2.	Disruption in Routine Family Activities	3.31 (1.578)	3.05 (1.477)	2.71 (1.165)	2.6958†
3.	Family Leisure	5.10 (1.231)	5.18 (1.295)	4.96 (1.288)	0.4431†
4.	Family Interaction	1.93 (1.177)	2.16 (1.209)	1.96 (0.973)	0.7551†
5.	Mental Health	0.26 (0.578)	0.26 (0.578)	0.20 (0.480)	0.2960†
6.	Physical Health	1.93 (0.445)	1.95 (0.340)	1.86 (0.430)	0.6996†
7.	Subjective Burden	1.18 (0.390)	1.21 (0.415)	1.18 (0.390)	0.1398†
8.	FBS Total	20.08 (4.570)	19.65 (3.820)	18.56 (4.330)	2.0220†

† indicates not significant

disruption of routine family activities was higher than those of other two groups, whereas Sequeira et al., (1990) in their study found that there was no significant difference in the perceived burden by mothers with reference to the sex of the child where as significant differences were found by way of disruption of routine family activities when degree of retardation was taken into account. Mothers perceived severely retarded children with larger number of associated problems like behaviour problems, seizures, poor comprehension, drooling of saliva etcetra as more disruptive for routine family activities. Similar results were reported by Moroney (1981), Narayanan (1979) and Seth (1979).

Tangri and Verma (1992) reported that mothers of mentally handicapped children reported higher social burden than those of physically handicapped children. Same authors reported that mothers of female mentally handicapped children more often reported burden because of disruption in family leisure and effect on mental health. Majority of the mothers rated the overall burden as moderate to severe.

When the mean values of perceived financial burden in the Table 5.12 are observed, fathers perceived more financial burden than the (the means being $\overline{X}_1 = 6.35$; $\overline{X}_2 = 5.83$ and $\overline{X}_3 = 5.66$ respectively) other two groups. Although these differences narrowly missed the required level of significance the trend is clear. Sequeria et al., (1990) stated that more than 50 per cent of the mothers of MHC had reported severe financial burden and Jain and Satyavathi (1969) reported that 61 per cent of the parents studied by them had financial constraints. Earlier studies on families of mentally handicapped children have reported financial burden in raising such children because of two reasons. One is additional expenditure involved in caring for a mentally handicapped child and the other one is reduced income because parents may have to spend extra time in parenting this child. Richards and McIntosh, (1973), Holroyd (1974), McAndrew (1976), Seth (1979), Veena (1985) and Dupont (1986). On the dimension of financial burden the third group significant other persons secured the least score ($\overline{X}_3 =$ 5.66). It is understandable that the family members in this group are not the sole care-providers and their role comes only next to the parents. Even though it is financially burdensome to the family to raise mentally handicapped children, this group did not feel the financial pinch as much as the parents did.

Family leisure is affected by the presence of mentally handicapped child. When the mean values on this dimension are observed, it is clear that mothers perceived it more burdensome, than the other two groups, since they are the ones who have to take care of the child day in and day out. Naturally their leisure time gets reduced, because of the extra care taking demands involved in raising a MHC.

Table 5.13 : Means and SDs of Various Scores as Perceived by the Respondents of Those Families with MHC

S.No.	Variable	Father n=60 M (σ)	Mother n=60 M (σ)	SOPs n=60 M (σ)	F
1.	Family Coping Skills	21.33 (1.590)	20.60 (1.509)	21.68 (1.845)	6.6950**
2.	Family Integration	7.78 (1.222)	7.78 (1.341)	7.98 (1.241)	0.4964†
3.	Family Satisfaction	25.21 (3.405)	24.53 (4.094)	25.60 (4.295)	1.1229†
4.	Behaviour Problems	3.85 (0.917)	3.83 (0.866)	3.88 (0.922)	0.477†

† indicates not significant
** indicates significant at 0.01 level of probability

Significant difference is observed in the perceptions of three categories of respondents with regard to their family coping skills as F value is 6.6956. Significant other persons scored higher (M=21.68) than the other two groups. (Fathers' Mean Score = 21.33 and Mothers' Mean Score = 20.60). This difference might be due to the fact that mothers need to attend to the unusual care giving demands of mentally handicapped children and management of daily needs of these children which is often stressful. They may find that their existing coping skills are insufficient to meet the additional demands. This is reflected in the observation that mothers got least score in coping skills when compared to the other two groups namely fathers and significant other persons.

Frey, Fewell and Vadasy (1989) found that cognitive coping factors (e.g. problem solving skills) were more important to the adjustment of fathers than to mothers of infants and toddlers with disabilities.

In two-parent households, poorer maternal coping scores were associated with higher level of father's education (Cullen et al., 1991). Because fathers' education is strongly associated in most studies with SES it appears that threats to that status or life style may exacerbate coping problems of the primary care taker who is usually the mother. Interesting is the presence of an older father seems to be supportive of mother's coping skills. Mother's usual coping strategies identified were talking and praying, while they reported their spouses coped by keeping busy and praying.

ANOVA results presented in Table 5.14 do not indicate any significant differences in the perceptions of three groups of respon-

Table 5.14 : Means and SDs of Family Functioning Scores as Perceived by the Respondents of Those Families with MHC

S.No.	Variable	Father n=60 M (σ)	Mother n=60 M (σ)	SOPs n=60 M (σ)	F
1.	Physical Care Function	16.15 (5.414)	17.65 (4.943)	17.05 (4.666)	1.3585†
2.	Leisure and Recoupera-tion	17.15 (2.543)	17.41 (2.533)	16.81 (2.432)	0.8652†
3.	Economic Function	18.71 (3.092)	19.13 (3.121)	19.23 (2.824)	0.4952†
4.	Love and Affection	10.18 ((1.096)	10.516 (1.308)	10.18 (1.346)	1.4103†
5.	Educational Function	4.26 (2.760)	3.93 (2.342)	4.21 (2.491)	0.3011†
6.	Guidance	10.08 (2.279)	10.13 (2.303)	10.18 (2.029)	0.0309†
7.	Vocational Function	27.61 (3.631)	27.90 (3.245)	27.86 (3.186)	0.1280†
8.	Socialization	32.78 (3.440)	32.40 (3.513)	31.98 (3.321)	0.8187†
9.	Self Definition	6.55 (2.554)	6.16 (0.693)	6.31 (1.534)	0.7176†
10.	FFS Total	143.50 (18.277)	145.23 (17.552)	143.86 (16.179)	0.1659†

† indicates not significant

dents namely fathers, mothers and significant other persons about the impact of MHC on family functioning. On the whole mothers secured a higher score than the other two groups in many dimensions of family functioning scale as well as the total score which indicate that mothers perception of the effect of MHC on family functioning is greater when compared with the other two groups of respondents.

Though the differences in the perceptions of three groups of respondents viz., fathers, mothers and significant other persons are statistically not significant, a close look at the mean values indicate some interesting facts.

Mothers' perception of the impact of MHC on different dimensions of family functioning is greater than that of the other groups except on three dimensions, like educational function, socialization and self-definition. The possible reason may be that mothers are not fully aware of the educational function of the family and may restrict themselves to the care giving and providing functions.

On the whole the perceptions of the three groups of respondents on all dimensions of family functioning appear more or less the same, thereby indicating that the impact of MHC on family functioning was felt in a similar way (The mean scores of the three groups of respondents were fathers = 143.50; mothers = 145.23 and for significant other persons = 143.86).

Our hypothesis is that the perceptions on the impact of MHC on family functioning of the three groups of respondents differ significantly. However the ANOVA results reveal that they differ significantly in their perceptions about personal health, marital issues, extended family support, personal resources, marital resources, disruption of routine family activities and family coping skills. The part of hypothesis concerning these variables is accepted. The remaining part of the hypothesis is rejected as the perception did not differ significantly.

Section–IV
Correlational Analysis

The next step was to study the association among different independent variables and their relation to the dependent variable.

All possible matrices of correlation were calculated by considering different combinations of variables along with their dimensions. An observation into these correlation matrices discloses the strength of the relationship between the dependent variable viz., impact of MHC on family functioning and the bunch independent variables and the different dimensions of independent variables. This type of analysis is useful to select the independent variables or their dimensions to predict the dependent variable by explaining the maximum possible variance in the dependent variable. Moreover the correlational analysis is also useful to identify the most significant variables which could influence the dependent variable. As usual the correlational matrices for fathers, mothers and significant other persons are presented in the following pages.

Fathers' Perceptions

From the correlation matrix it is clear that the strength of relationship between the impact of mentally handicapped child on family functioning and socio-economic status is significant at 0.01 level and the highest (about 47%) among all. The dimensions of SES viz., material status and non-material status are also possessing significant relationship but the strength is little less than the total SES (43% and 45% respectively).

Research findings concerning the responses of parents of handicapped children from different socio-economic categories are contradictory. (Minnes, 1986). There are a few studies which indicated the buffering role of SES on the stressful effects of raising children with disabilities.

Socio-economic status predicted significant amounts of variance for only 3 of the 15 scales in QRS-F viz., Lack of family integration, limits on family opportunity and financial problems (Dunst et al., 1986). In another research reported by Minnes (1988) Socio-economic status could predict 10 per cent of the variance in terminal illness stress and 24 per cent of the variance in financial stress.

Salisbury (1990) used annual family income as a demographic variable and found significant correlations between family income and child's characteristics, family disharmony and financial stress.

SES/Family income did not exert significant effect on paren-

Table 5.15 : Intercorrelations of Independent Variables and their Dimensions with the Dependent Variable as Perceived by Fathers

Variable	SES	FR	FCS	FIS	FB	FS	BP	MS	MMS	SR	PR	MR	FF
SES	1.000	--	--	--	--	--	--	--	--	--	--	--	--
FR	0.134†	1.000	--	--	--	--	--	--	--	--	--	--	--
FCS	0.159†	–0.051†	1.000	--	--	--	--	--	--	--	--	--	--
FIS	0.256*	0.054†	–0.070†	1.000	--	--	--	--	--	--	--	--	--
FB	0.167†	–0.133†	0.118†	–0.185†	1.000	--	--	--	--	--	--	--	--
FS	0.355**	–0.047†	–0.082†	0.138†	–0.283*	1.000	--	--	--	--	--	--	--
BP	–0.055†	0.306*	–0.070†	–0.181†	–0.054†	–0.044†	1.000	--	--	--	--	--	--
MS	0.950**	0.072†	–0.1000†	0.151†	–0.120†	0.361**	0.003†	1.000	--	--	--	--	--
NMS	0.940**	0.185†	0.205†	0.339**	–0.199†	0.307*	–0.112†	0.786**	1.000	--	--	--	--
SR	–0.147†	0.810**	0.074†	–0.061†	0.013†	–0.253*	0.246†	–0.187†	–0.087†	1.000	--	--	--
PR	0.404**	0.332**	–0.034†	0.151†	0.100†	0.174†	0.160†	0.353**	0.143†	–0.090†	1.0000	--	--
MR	0.103†	0.313*	–0.196†	0.102†	–0.220†	0.164†	0.035†	0.101†	0.093†	0.011†	–0.230†	1.000	--
FF	0.468**	–0.152†	0.260*	0.068†	0.191†	0.388**	0.346**	0.435**	0.451**	–0.339**	0.217†	0.026†	1.000

Table Values : 0.05 0.250; 0.01 0.325

Note : † indicates not significant

* indicates significant at 0.05 level of probability ** indicates significant at 0.01 level of probability

tal response to a developmentally disabled child. (Beckman, 1983; Flynt and Wood, 1989; Friedrich, 1979; Sletzer and Krauss, 1989).

Glidden (1993) concluded that SES/Income is related to what is labelled as "financial problems" or "financial stress".

A retrospective study by Grossman (1972) found that siblings from higher SES families were relatively protected from the adverse consequences of having a retarded sibling.

The correlation matrix in the present study indicates that there is a high positive correlation between SES and the impact of mentally handicapped child on family functioning. Parents with high SES scores reflect higher education, greater understanding of the problems and risks associated with mental retardation. Parents' social values and social standing in addition to socio-economic class effect the ways in which they perceive mental retardation. Educated parents tend to have more difficulty in adjusting to what is perceived as the tragedy of "mental retardation" in their offspring (Dunlap and Hollingsworth, 1976; Farber, 1959, 1960; Garfield and Helper, 1962; Holt, 1958; Levinson, 1975; Weller et al., 1974). Most of the studies reported above lend support to the results of the present study with regard to SES and the impact of MHC on family functioning.

Of course the inter-correlations between SES and its dimensions reveal the same idea. Among the other independent variables which are possessing a positive and significant inter-correlations with SES are Personal resources (40%), Family satisfaction (35%) and Family integration (25%). Thus the influence of SES along with the other inter-correlated variables may be significant on the impact of MHC on family functioning.

The next most significant set of variables influencing the impact of MHC on family functioning are family satisfaction and behaviour problems. The strengths of relationship are about 39 per cent and 35 per cent respectively. The fact that family satisfaction is associated with the impact of MHC on family functioning appears conflicting and contradictory. In a normal course family satisfaction should contribute for better family functioning through buffering the stressful effects associated with the rearing and management of MHC. If family satisfaction is not associated with better family performance, may be, it can be understood that better family functioning may lead to family satisfaction. So, family satisfaction is the consequential effect of better family functioning.

It is natural for some individuals to exaggerate the negative things even though they are endowed with many other positive things in the other domains of life. So, mental retardation associated with social stigma may appear a tragedy in their life even though they have the utmost family satisfaction.

Regarding behaviour problems, Bradshaw and Lawton (1978) reported that behaviour problems associated with mental retardation impose extra care-taking demands and burden parents.

Beckman and Bell (1981) stated that serious behaviour problems contribute to parental stress and rejection.

Friedrich et al., (1985) summarized that child variables viz., behaviour problems and medical problems as related to greater parent and family problems.

The stress on family members tend to increase with the presence of behaviour problems in the mentally handicapped children (Byrne and Cunningham, 1985).

Because of the behaviour problems MHC are not socially accepted (Gardner, 1971, Eyman and Call, 1977). All the above mentioned evidence render support to the present finding that behaviour problems create stress in parents and thus impede the normal family functioning. Behaviour problems were strong predictors of parenting stress in both the age groups viz., pre-school as well as middle childhood groups (Orr et al., 1990).

Fifty (50) per cent of the variance in explaining stress was accounted to perceptions of parents about dependence and behaviour problems of the child (Baxter, 1992). However a significant but negative correlation coefficient is found between the impact of MHC on family functioning and social resources. This means social resources which include community facilities, interactions with close friends, and neighbours and participation in associations may render help to the fathers directly or indirectly in performing the family functions. In other words the perceptions of fathers indicate that the social resources dilute the impact of MHC on family functioning. However, the family resources as a whole (personal, social and marital resources) as an independent variable could not exhibit any association with father's perceptions of the impact of MHC on family functioning.

The last variable which is positively and significantly associated (at 0.05 level) with the impact of MHC on family functioning is family coping skills as perceived by fathers. Contrary to the present finding that better coping skills are associated with greater impact of MHC on family functioning, Frey, Greenberg and Fewell (1989) reported that positive self-appraisals of coping skills were related significantly to lower parental stress, better family adjustment, and less psychological distress for both parents of young children with disabilities.

Thus, out of the seven independent variables, SES, family coping skills, family satisfaction and behaviour problems could significantly influence the impact of MHC on family functioning, whereas the other three variables namely family resources, family integration and perception of family burden did not exhibit statistically significant relationship. But the dimensions of these variables may have their influence on the impact of MHC on family functioning. The following Tables depict the correlation matrices of the various dimensions of each variable and the impact of MHC on family functioning.

Among the seven independent variables included in the study SES appeared to be the most significant variable associated with the impact of MHC on family functioning (r=0.468). But an observation into the above Table reveals that material possessions of the family exhibit the strongest relationship (51%) with the impact of MHC on family functioning than any other dimensions of SES. Occupational status is the next important variable which relates to the impact of MHC on family functioning, the strength of relationship being 50 per cent. Material possessions acquired by the family, and elevated occupational status together keep the family on the highest rung of the ladder in the social hierarchy. Such a family enjoys an elevated status in the society. The presence of MHC in such a family is usually taken as a curse and naturally it will be very difficult to adjust with the situation. So the impact of MHC is felt to a greater extent in families with elevated socio-economic status.

Family type is another important dimension of SES which influenced the impact of MHC on family functioning (r = 0.40).

Table 5.16 : Intercorrelations of SES and its Components with the Dependent Variable as Perceived by Fathers

Variable	C	OC	ED	SP	L	H	FP	MP	FT	SF	FF
C	1.000	--	--	--	--	--	--	--	--	--	--
OC	0.653**	1.000	--	--	--	--	--	--	--	--	--
ED	0.718**	0.640**	1.000	--	--	--	--	--	--	--	--
SP	0.233†	0.238†	0.230†	1.000	--	--	--	--	--	--	--
L	0.516**	0.774**	0.537**	0.311*	1.000	--	--	--	--	--	--
H	0.675**	0.667**	0.706**	0.363**	0.748**	1.000	--	--	--	--	--
FP	0.427**	0.716**	0.371**	0.367**	0.735**	0.578**	1.000	--	--	--	--
MP	0.612**	0.692**	0.518**	0.345**	0.671**	0.644**	0.717**	1.000	--	--	--
FT	0.299*	0.412**	0.213†	0.111†	0.299*	0.169†	0.412**	0.487**	1.000	--	--
SF	0.075†	0.211†	–0.019†	0.000†	0.247†	0.035†	0.300*	0.069†	0.444**	1.000	--
FF	0.346**	0.499**	0.357**	0.046†	0.311*	0.372**	0.336**	00.512**	0.400**	–0.087†	1.000

Note : † indicates not significant
* indicates significant at 0.05 level of probability
** indicates significant at 0.01 level of probability

But the size of the family is found to be an insignificant variable influencing the impact of MHC on family functioning. Although the direction of the relationship is negative, this sort of a relationship indicates, that as the family size increased the impact of mentally handicapped child may not be felt very much, which may be due to the availability of more number of people to attend to the extra care taking demands of MHC.

Conflicting evidence is available about the impact of family size on stress. Family size is related to increased parent and family stress (Friedrich, Wilturner and Cohen, 1985; Kazak and Marvin, 1984; Noa et al., 1989; Singer and Farkas, 1989; and Turnbull and Turnbull, 1986). In discussing the inter correlationships between family size and stress Turnbull and Turnbull pointed out that in larger families, a greater atmosphere of normalcy is found and that siblings are available to help and to absorb some parental expectations for achievement thus reducing the feeling of stress.

Among the remaining dimensions of SES except social participation all others possess a significant and positive correlation with the impact of MHC on family functioning whereas social participation exhibits a significant negative correlation. This might be because when people participate in social gatherings the extra stress and strain involved in caring for a mentally handicapped child may be reduced. Social isolation in families of mentally retarded children is an often reported finding (Carver and Carver, 1992; Davis and McKay, 1973; Dunlop and Hollingsworth, 1974; Farber, 1959, 1960, 1964, Hot, 1958; Jacobs, 1974; Legaay and Keough, 1966; Levinson, 1975; McAllister et al., 1973; Mayerwitz and Farber, 1966; and Schonnel and Watts, 1956). McDowell and Gabel (1981) found significantly smaller networks for parents of mentally retarded children as compared to a contrast group of parents of normal children. The reason for this type of social isolation may be that families may be too emotionally and physically exhausted to maintain ties with friends and relatives. Another reason might be, the stigma attached to mental retardation. In the present study fathers who had a higher score on social participation did not perceive much impact of MHC on family functioning which is obvious.

It was found that the total family resources could not significantly be associated with the impact of MHC on family functioning (r=–0.152, vide Table 5.17). However, "social resources" was found to be a significant variable exercising its association with the impact of MHC on family functioning. But it is clear from the above correlation matrix, that two types of resources namely; positive beliefs and close friends could significantly (P>0.05) be associated with the impact of MHC on family functioning. However, the relationship is positive between positive beliefs and the impact of MHC on family functioning while it is negative between close friends and the impact of MHC on family functioning.

Although the association between family resources and the impact of MHC on family functioning is not significant the relationship exists in a negative direction. This indicates that as the total family resources score increases the impact of MHC on family functioning gets reduced. When "social resources" as an independent variable is considered, the correlation value (r=–0.339) was significant and negative, indicating greater the social resources, the lesser will be the impact of MHC on family functioning.

The other types of resources namely personal resources and marital resources could not exert any influence on the impact of MHC on family functioning. But the direction of relationship these dimensions with the dependent variable discloses that out of eight dimensions five dimensions possess negative relationship and the remaining three dimensions are positively related to the impact of MHC on family functioning. However, two dimensions viz., social interactions and participation in associations are not included in the correlation matrix as the scores obtained on these two dimensions by all the respondents were found to be the same.

Although the correlation between the impact of mentally handicapped child on family functioning and family burden was not significant (r=0.191, P<0.05) the above matrix discloses that two components of family burden scale viz., family leisure and physical health are significantly associated with the impact of MHC on family functioning. The strength of the relationships are about 37 per cent and 35 per cent respectively. Seth and Sitholey (1986) reported that parental burden with a mentally handicapped child in the form of interferences in their family routine or leisure and recreation which resulted in social, marital, familial and emotional problems in the home setting. Burden of care is usually more when the mentally handicapped child is kept at home. Parents are subjected to great

Table 5.17 : Intercorrelations of Family Resources and its Dimensions with the Dependent Variable as Perceived by Fathers

Variable	CR	PH	PSS	PB	MI	EF	CF	N	FF
CR	1.000	--	--	--	--	--	--	--	--
PH	–0.093†	1.000	--	--	--	--	--	--	--
PSS	–0.005†	0.122†	1.000	--	--	--	--	--	--
PB	–0.031†	0.006†	0.068†	1.000	--	--	--	--	--
MI	–0.122†	0.017†	–0.231†	0.083†	1.000	--	--	--	--
EF	–0.125†	–0.321*	–0.145†	–0.052†	–0.157†	1.000	--	--	--
CF	0.264*	–0.158†	0.078†	–0.077†	0.051†	0.134†	1.000	--	--
N	0.117†	–0.192†	0.237†	–0.142†	–0.016†	0.169†	0.388**	1.000	--
FF	–0.152†	0.074†	–0.071†	0.306*	–0.214†	0.128†	–0.271*	–0.173†	1.000

Note : † indicates not significant
* indicates significant at 0.05 level of probability
** indicates significant at 0.01 level of probability

physical as well as psychological stress in day to day management. As a result the parents get exhausted and the burden of care is reflected in a higher score on burden related to physical health. So fathers perceived that burden due to their mentally handicapped children is more in two dimensions of burden scale namely leisure and physical health. Leisure time is very much restricted in families with a MHC due to extra care-taking demands.

Thus out of the seven independent variables included in the study, three variables are comprised of different components/ dimensions and the remaining four are represented with the single scores. To predict the impact of MHC on family functioning it is proposed to treat the components of these complex variables as independent variables. However, similar analysis has to be carried on the perceptions of mothers and significant other persons before presenting the summary of step-wise multiple regression analysis to predict the impact of MHC on family functioning.

Correlation Aspects (Mothers)

An observation into the above matrix reveals that the impact of MHC is highly correlated with social resources of the family (r = -0.485). As there is a negative correlation between the impact of MHC on family functioning and social resources it can be understood that with an increase in social resources the impact of MHC on family functioning gets reduced. In other words mothers perceived that social resources are helping in attending to the needs of the MHC, which is being reflected in reduced scores on the impact of MHC on family functioning. Of course fathers' perceptions about social resources are in line with those of mothers but the intensity of association between these two variables in the case of mothers is more.

Social resources include community facilities, frequency of contacts by close friends and neighbours, the intensity of these relationships and the degree of reciprocity and maintenance of these relationships overtime and the functions of these exchanges. Since the scores on these social resources reflect the mother's perceptions about social resources, they are more important than the actual social resources available. So a higher score on social resources dilutes the impact of MHC on family functioning. This might be the reason for a negative correlation between social resources and

Table 5.18 : Intercorrelations of Family Burden and its Dimensions with the Dependent Variable as Perceived by Fathers

Variable	FB	DRFA	FL	FI	MH	PH	SB	FF
FB	1.000	--	--	--	--	--	--	--
DRFA	0.202†	1.000	--	--	--	--	--	--
FL	0.403**	0.306*	1.000	--	--	--	--	--
FI	0.302*	0.276*	0.636**	1.000	--	--	--	--
MH	0.162†	0.203†	0.295*	0.176†	1.000	--	--	--
PH	0.292*	0.055†	0.383**	0.379**	0.399**	1.000	--	--
SB	0.027†	0.124†	–0.180†	–0.231†	0.005†	0.169†	1.000	--
FF	–0.211†	–0.208†	0.366**	0.190†	0.010†	0.349**	0.004†	1.000

Note : † indicates not significant
* indicates significant at 0.05 level of probability
** indicates significant at 0.01 level of probability

the impact of MHC on family functioning.

Moudgil et al., (1985) observed that those parents who were having cordial relations and received maximum social-emotional support from the spouse, parents, family members, relatives and friends experienced less stress and problems as compared to those who got little or minimum support.

Frey, Greenberg and Fewell (1989) found that mothers with more helpful, social support networks had better family adjustments whereas fathers who felt more criticism from their support networks had poorer family adjustment. Thus difference between intra-individual and inter-personal skills between mothers and fathers appear to be related to parental adaptation.

Krauss (1993) found that mothers were more affected by their social support networks than were fathers. Fathers may turn inward towards their families whereas mothers turn outward towards their social support networks in the face of a "crisis" regarding their child's development.

The next most important variable having a significantly high correlation with the impact of MHC on family functioning is Socio-Economic Status (SES). The strength of the relationship is 48 per cent. However the components of SES viz., Material status and Non-material status are possessing high positive correlation with the dependent variable but the strength is 45 per cent and 46 per cent respectively. This means that the total SES is capable of explaining more about the impact of MHC on family functioning than its components. The interpretation given in the case of fathers for the same type of relationship between SES and impact of MHC on family functioning holds good even with mothers..

The other significant variables having their association with the impact of MHC on family functioning are family satisfaction and family resources. Family satisfaction is positively correlated while family resources are negatively correlated. Both are significant at 0.05 level. Among the components of family resources social resources are significantly and negatively correlated, while the other two components personal resources and marital resources are not significantly associated.

The other variables which are not significantly correlated with

Table 5.19 : Intercorrelations of Independent Variables and their Dimensions with the Dependent Variable as Perceived by Mothers

Variable	SES	FR	FCS	FIS	FB	FS	BP	MS	MMS	SR	PR	MR	FF
SES	1.000	--	--	--	--	--	--	--	--	--	--	--	--
FR	–0.147†	1.000	--	--	--	--	--	--	--	--	--	--	--
FCS	–0.122†	–0.005†	1.000	--	--	--	--	--	--	--	--	--	--
FIS	–0.088†	–0.165†	–0.186†	1.000	--	--	--	--	--	--	--	--	--
FB	–0.102†	0.071†	–0.139†	–0.243†	1.000	--	--	--	--	--	--	--	--
FS	0.424**	–0.071†	–0.132†	0.213†	–0.197†	1.000	--	--	--	--	--	--	--
BP	–0.098†	0.164†	0.026†	–0.275*	–0.233†	–0.003†	1.000	--	--	--	--	--	--
MS	0.955**	–0.144†	–0.153†	0.058†	–0.078†	0.403**	0.011†	1.000	--	--	--	--	--
NMS	0.938**	–0.133†	–0.072†	0.113†	–0.119†	0.400**	–0.215†	0.793**	1.000	--	--	--	--
SR	–0.385**	0.722**	0.217†	–0.095†	0.188†	–0.118†	–0.058†	–0.360**	–0.371**	1.000	--	--	--
PR	0.158†	0.458**	–0.135†	–0.202†	–0.069†	–0.013†	0.279*	0.158†	0.139†	–0.159†	1.000	--	--
MR	0.173†	0.361**	–0.257†	0.107†	–0.113†	0.083†	–0.125†	0.136†	0.197†	0.050†	–0.090†	1.000	--
FF	0.480**	–0.288*	–0.128†	0.026†	–0.006†	0.318*	–0.246†	0.451**	0.458**	–0.485**	0.153†	0.007†	1.000

Note : † indicates not significant
* indicates significant at 0.05 level of probability
** indicates significant at 0.01 level of probability

the impact of MHC on family functioning are family coping skills, family integration and behaviour problems.

It is interesting to note that the variable 'behaviour problems' appear to be insignificant in affecting the impact of MHC on family functioning as perceived by mothers, whereas father's perception about behaviour problems is contrary. Dunst, Trivette and Deal (1988) stated that to the extent a negative behaviour is predictable and recurring even a serious behaviour problem may become fairly routine and minimally stressful.

The above mentioned study provides explanation for the results of the present study in the correlation between behaviour problems and the impact of MHC on family functioning is not significant in the case of mothers.

However it would be better to study the relationship between dependent variable and the components of SES scale, family resources scale and family burden scale.

Among the seven independent variables included in the study SES appeared to be the most significantly correlated variable (r=0.480). But a perusal of the above Table reveals occupational status of the family exhibiting the strongest relationship (52%) with the impact of MHC on family functioning than any other dimensions of SES. Material possessions is the next important variable which influences the family functioning. The strength of the relationship being (45%) land and family type are other important dimensions influencing the impact of MHC on family functioning. Both the variables have equal strength of relationship (40%).

The other dimensions which had significant and positive influence on the impact of MHC on family functioning are house, farm power and caste. The remaining dimensions in SES viz., education, social participation and size of the family are found to be insignificant in changing the impact of MHC on family functioning.

It is interesting to note that family type exhibits a positive correlation with the impact of MHC on family functioning whereas size of the family had a negative correlation though it is not significant. These two correlations appear to be contradictory and need to be understood keeping the typical interactional patterns

Table 5.20 : Intercorrelations of SES and its Components with the Dependent Variable as Perceived by Mothers

Variable	C	OC	ED	SP	L	H	FP	MP	FT	SF	FF
C	1.000	--	--	--	--	--	--	--	--	--	--
OC	0.502**	1.000	--	--	--	--	--	--	--	--	--
ED	0.535**	0.414**	1.000	--	--	--	--	--	--	--	--
SP	0.018†	0.109†	0.250†	1.000	--	--	--	--	--	--	--
L	0.516**	0.777**	0.556**	0.242†	1.000	--	--	--	--	--	--
H	0.662**	0.570**	0.642**	0.316*	0.751**	1.000	--	--	--	--	--
FP	0.407**	0.628**	0.289*	0.211†	0.713**	0.573**	1.000	--	--	--	--
MP	0.598**	0.592**	0.340**	0.174†	0.620**	0.608**	0.703**	1.000	--	--	--
FT	0.299*	0.416**	0.067†	0.135†	0.299*	0.195†	0.419**	0.483**	1.000	--	--
SF	0.147†	0.183†	–0.029†	0.073†	0.259*	0.073†	0.332*	0.178†	0.469**	1.000	--
FF	0.341**	0.524**	0.188†	0.021†	0.399**	0.379**	0.354**	0.446**	0.399**	0.058†	1.000

Note : † indicates not significant
* indicates significant at 0.05 level of probability
** indicates significant at 0.01 level of probability

seen in nuclear as well as joint families. Even though number of family members in a joint family are generally more compared to a nuclear family, the size of the joint family does not exhibit the same correlation with the impact of MHC on family functioning as it does in a nuclear family. So it is not the actual number of people available for the care of MHC but the relationship of such people to the target child which is more important in reducing the impact of MHC on family functioning.

It was evident that the variable "family resource" is negatively correlated with the impact of MHC on family functioning (r=–0.288, vide Table 5.19). But it is clear from the above correlation matrix that close friends had a significantly high correlation with the impact of MHC on family functioning. The strength of the relationship is 61 per cent and the relationship is negative.

As Crnic and Greenberg (1990) reported that emotional support from friends is better than that from husbands in reducing the adverse effects of daily hassles of parenting. Since mothers usually share their experiences of hassles with children's behaviour with their friends, these interactions help in reducing the parenting stress. So when interactions with close friends are better and more the impact of mentally handicapped child on family functioning was not felt by mothers.

The other two types of resources which had significant association with the impact of MHC on family functioning are; problem solving skills and positive beliefs. However the relationship is negative between problem solving skills and the impact of MHC on family functioning while it is positive between positive beliefs and the impact of MHC on family functioning. It is understandable that when individuals possess problem solving skills, an important dimension of human resource, they will be in a better position to tackle the problems associated with their MHC. Naturally the impact of such children on family functioning may not be felt very much, when family members possess the necessary problem solving skills. Frey, Greenberg and Fewell (1989) found that positive self appraisals of coping skills were related significantly to lower parental stress, better family adjustment and less psychological distress for both mothers and fathers of young children with disabilities. The results of earlier studies lend support to present finding about positive beliefs. Beliefs in religion has not generally been found to

Table 5.21 : Intercorrelations of Family Resources and its Dimensions with the Dependent Variable as Perceived by Mothers

Variable	CR	PH	PSS	PB	MI	EF	CF	N	FF
CR	1.000	--	--	--	--	--	--	--	--
PH	–0.025†	1.000	--	--	--	--	--	--	--
PSS	–0.054†	–0.074†	1.000	--	--	--	--	--	--
PB	–0.048†	0.118†	0.072†	1.000	--	--	--	--	--
MI	–0.011†	0.041†	–0.142†	0.085†	1.000	--	--	--	--
EF	–0.090†	–0.139†	0.195†	–0.020†	–0.526**	1.000	--	--	--
CF	0.016†	–0.169†	0.290*	–0.397**	0.019†	0.119†	1.000	--	--
N	0.105†	–0.024†	0.095†	–0.160†	–0.336**	0.329**	0.486**	1.000	--
FF	–0.166†	0.151†	–0.261*	0.252*	–0.228†	0.184†	–0.607**	–0.085†	1.000

Note : † indicates not significant
* indicates significant at 0.05 level of probability
** indicates significant at 0.01 level of probability

Table 5.22 : Intercorrelations of Family Burden and its Dimensions with the Dependent Variable as Perceived by Mothers

Variable	FB	DRFA	FL	FI	MH	PH	SB	FF
FB	1.000	--	--	--	--	--	--	--
DRFA	0.034†	1.000	--	--	--	--	--	--
FL	0.479**	0.128†	1.000	--	--	--	--	--
FI	0.341**	0.185†	0.078†	1.000	--	--	--	--
MH	0.088†	0.143†	0.069†	–0.065†	1.000	--	--	--
PH	–0.146†	–0.029†	–0.017†	–0.062†	–0.017†	1.000	--	--
SB	0.047†	–0.156†	0.019†	–0.107†	–0.174†	0.078†	1.000	--
FF	0.140†	–0.185†	0.086†	–0.020†	–0.217†	–0.009†	0.074†	1.000

Note : † indicates not significant
** indicates significant at 0.01 level of probability

contribute to family adjustment (Friedrich, 1979; German and Maisto, 1982; and Waisbern, 1982), although earlier research has described a significant relationship between religious beliefs and whether or not MHC were cared for at home (Farber, 1959; Zuk, 1959).

The family's beliefs and perceptions about mental handicap may determine the coping strategies, the families evolve and in turn may be modified by the particular strategies used (Crnic et al., 1983; and Turnbull et al., 1984).

The other types of resources/dimensions could not influence the impact of MHC on family functioning. But the direction of the relationship of these dimensions, with the dependent variable discloses that out of eight dimensions, five are showing negative relationship and the remaining three dimensions are positively related to the impact of MHC on family functioning. Hence it may be inferred that majority of the dimensions of family resources weaken the impact of MHC on family functioning.

Though the correlation between family burden and the impact of MHC on family functioning is not significant ($r=-0.006$; $P<0.05$) it was planned to find out whether the dimensions of family burden had any significant association with the impact of MHC on family functioning. A separate correlation matrix has been developed. It is evident from the above matrix that none of the dimensions had correlation with the dependent variable.

Correlation Aspects of Significant other Persons (SOPs)

The composition of SOPs includes grandparents from both maternal and paternal side and uncles and aunts in a similar manner. It also includes the siblings of the target child. This situation of relatives living with the families of MHC and participating in family activities is typical of rural Indian families. The heterogeneity in the composition of this group may be kept in mind while trying to interpret the correlation analysis of dependent and independent variables for SOPs.

From the correlation matrix, it is evident, that the impact of MHC on family functioning is highly correlated with marital resources ($r=0.513$). The strength of the relationship is 51 per cent and it is significant at 0.01 level.

Table 5.23 : Intercorrelations of Independent Variables and their Dimensions with the Dependent Variable as Perceived by SOPs

Variable	SES	FR	FCS	FIS	FB	FS	BP	MS	MMS	SR	PR	MR	FF
SES	1.000	--	--	--	--	--	--	--	--	--	--	--	--
FR	0.184†	1.000	--	--	--	--	--	--	--	--	--	--	--
FCS	0.225†	0.190†	1.000	--	--	--	--	--	--	--	--	--	--
FIS	0.085†	0.264*	0.123†	1.000	--	--	--	--	--	--	--	--	--
FB	0.131†	–0.092†	–0.132†	–0.042†	1.000	--	--	--	--	--	--	--	--
FS	0.207†	0,124†	0.067†	0.186†	–0.001†	1.000	--	--	--	--	--	--	--
BP	–0.067†	0.265*	–0.122†	–0.017†	–0.076†	–0.205†	1.000	--	--	--	--	--	--
MS	0.933**	0.075†	0.081†	0.100†	–0.165†	0.236†	0.001†	1.000	--	--	--	--	--
NMS	0.883**	0.288*	0.367**	0.258*	–0.059†	0.127†	–0.143†	0.655**	1.000	--	--	--	--
SR	–0.171†	0.690**	–0.021†	0.210†	0.051†	–0.055†	–0.296*	–0.229†	–0.060†	1.000	--	--	--
PR	0.357**	0.699**	0.370**	0.226†	–0.207†	–0.173†	0.326**	0.239†	0.438**	0.353**	1.0000	--	--
MR	0.254*	0.395**	0.074†	0.038†	–0.063†	0.152†	–0.144†	0.223†	0.241†	–0.262*	–0.030†	1.000	--
FF	0.440**	–0.029†	0.095†	–0.122†	0.188†	0.367**	–0.411**	0.425**	0.370**	–0.466**	0.003†	0.513**	1.000

Note : † indicates not significant
* indicates significant at 0.05 level of probability
** indicates significant at 0.01 level of probability

Marital resources include support from the spouse as well as support from extended family members. Families without much financial resources and access to formal service systems in order to survive must rely heavily on informal support networks. The kin systems of poor and lower middle class families are often extraordinarily strong and supportive. In families of mentally retarded children frequent contacts with grandmothers are especially significant in increasing coping ability. (Farber, 1960; Hot, 1958; and Waisbern, 1980).

The variable 'marital resources' is significantly and positively correlated with the impact of MHC on family functioning. This finding appears conflicting and contradictory. If the composition of this group of respondents namely SOPs is observed more than 50 per cent of them were relatives from paternal side (refer Table 5.6). The reactions of relatives from the paternal side to the birth of a MHC are not always palatable to the family. Most often the mother of MHC is considered to be responsible for the birth of the defective child and blamed. Even though relatives from paternal side come forward to help the family with a MHC, the bickerings, the criticism, victimization and other reactions may not facilitate healthy family functioning. This might explain the reason for a high positive correlation between resources and the impact of MHC on family functioning in Indian cultural set up.

The next most significant variables influencing the impact of MHC on family functioning are "social resources", "socio-economic status", "material status" and "behaviour problems". The strength of the relationships are about 47 per cent, 44 per cent, 43 per cent and 41 per cent respectively. The relationship between behaviour problems and the dependent variable is in negative direction whereas the other three variables had a positive relationship.

Social resources just like SES could not reduce the impact of MHC on family functioning as perceived by SOPs. But there is plenty of research evidence available to indicate the buffering effect of these two variables in reducing stress. "Social Resources" as one dimension of family resources exhibit a significant and positive relationship with the impact of MHC on family functioning. Social support has a demonstrated buffering effect, i.e., high stress families with high social support cope better than do similarly stressed families with low social support. Low-stress families do equally well with or without peer social support. The relationship is interactive in that better coppers presumably have more social support and more social support facilitates coping (Johnson & Sarson, 1978). On the contrary Dunst and Trivett (1988) reported that social support has more powerful influence in inter-personal behaviour than it does on family functioning. There is considerable evidence indicating that social support is a powerful mediator of personal well-being (Dunst, Trivette and Cross, 1986) and family adjustment (McCubbin et al., 1980).

The last variables which are positively and significantly (0.01 level) associated with the impact of MHC on family functioning are "non-material status" and "family satisfaction". The remaining variables viz., family resources, family coping skills, family integration, family burden and personal resources, are not significantly correlated with the impact of MHC on family functioning. Non-material status is one of the dimensions of SES which includes, caste, occupation, education, social participation, family type and family size. This variable non-material status is positively and significantly correlated with the impact of MHC on family functioning according to the perceptions of SOPs. The place of the family in the social ladder is decided by non-material status. It is difficult for individuals with a high non-material status score to accept a child with mental handicap. When MHC is not accepted in the family, the difficulties and problems associated with the management of such a child are compounded and the impact is felt to a greater extent.

Significant other persons perceived that behaviour problems seen in MHC are negatively and significantly correlated with the impact of MHC on family functioning. It may be because that this group of respondents who are other than natural parents may perceive that their presence in the family is a valuable human resource in abating the stressful effects resulted because of the child's behaviour problems. Moreover multiple parenting by this group of respondents viz., significant other persons in family has a facilitating effect. Besides parents, other adult figures exert a positive influence by way of devoting certain amount of time. So the impact of behaviour problems might not have reflected in the family functioning scores as it happened with fathers. The dimen-

Table 5.24 : Intercorrelations of SES and its Components with the Dependent Variable as Perceived by SOPs

Variable	C	OC	ED	SP	L	H	FP	MP	FT	SF	FF
C	1.000	--	--	--	--	--	--	--	--	--	--
OC	0.627**	1.000	--	--	--	--	--	--	--	--	--
ED	0.075†	–0.026†	1.000	--	--	--	--	--	--	--	--
SP	–0.082†	0.040†	0.229†	1.000	--	--	--	--	--	--	--
L	0.499**	0.694**	0.093†	0.081†	1.000	--	--	--	--	--	--
H	0.607**	0.594**	0.208†	0.163†	0.752**	1.000	--	--	--	--	--
FP	0.415**	0.711**	0.045†	0.096†	0.712**	0.584**	1.000	--	--	--	--
MP	0.595**	0.641**	–0.036†	0.088†	0.622**	0.650**	0.705**	1.000	--	--	--
FT	0.316*	0.396**	–0.298*	–0.123†	0.251*	0.204†	0.261*	0.419**	1.000	--	--
SF	0.210†	0.186†	–0.051†	0.027†	0.086†	0.084†	0.128†	0.261†	0.419**	1.000	--
FF	0.289*	0.522**	–0.017†	0.185†	0.370**	0.395**	0.326**	0.326**	0.410**	0.366**	1.000

Note : † indicates not significant
* indicates significant at 0.05 level of probability
** indicates significant at 0.01 level of probability

sions of other independent variables may have their influence on the impact of MHC on family functioning. The following Tables depict the correlation matrices of the various dimensions of each variable and family functioning.

Among the seven independent variables include in the study SES appeared to be one of the significant variable influencing family functioning (r = 0.440). But an observation of the above Table makes it clear that occupational status of the family exhibits strongest relationship (52%) with the impact of MHC on family functioning than any other dimension of SES. Family type is the next important variable which influences family functioning (r=0.410). House and land are the next significant variables in influencing family functioning. The strength of the relationships are 40 per cent and 37 per cent respectively. Size of the family is the next significantly correlated variable with family functioning (r=0.366). Farm power and material possessions have equal strength of relationship (33%) in influencing the impact of MHC on family functioning followed by Caste (29%). The remaining two dimensions in SES viz., education and social participation are found to be insignificant variables in influencing the impact of MHC on family functioning although the direction of relationship of education and the other one is negative.

It was found that family resources could not significantly influence the impact of MHC on family functioning (r=–0.029; vide Table 5.23). But, it is clear from the above correlation matrix that close friends emerged as the most significantly correlated variable with the impact of MHC on family functioning. The strength of the relationship is 51 per cent and the direction of relationship is negative. The next important variable having high correlation with the impact of MHC on family functioning is "marital issues" (r=0.438). The other types of resources which had significant correlation with family functioning are 'extended family', 'community resources' and 'neighbours'. The strengths of relationship are 36 per cent, 28 per cent and 26 per cent respectively. The direction of relationship between community resources and impact of MHC on family functioning is negative while it is positive with 'extended family' and 'neighbours'. However, the remaining resources (dimensions) viz., 'personal health', 'problem solving skills' and 'positive beliefs' could not influence the impact of MHC

Table 5.25 : Intercorrelations of Family Resources and its Dimensions with the Dependent Variable as Perceived by SOPs

Variable	CR	PH	PSS	PB	MI	EF	CF	N	FF
CR	1.000	--	--	--	--	--	--	--	--
PH	-0.259*	1.000	--	--	--	--	--	--	--
PSS	0.081†	-0.018†	1.000	--	--	--	--	--	--
PB	-0.077†	-0.006†	0.065†	1.000	--	--	--	--	--
MI	0.113†	-0.313*	-0.272*	0.138†	1.000	--	--	--	--
EF	-0.06†	0.025†	0.179†	0.289*	0.216†	1.000	--	--	--
CF	0.069†	0.366**	0.462**	0.002†	-0.497**	-0.073†	1.000	--	--
N	-0.034†	0.018†	0.060†	0.343**	0.108†	0.181†	0.063†	1.000	--
FF	-0.279*	-0.210†	-0.057†	0.192†	0.438**	0.355**	-0.509**	0.257*	1.000

Note : † indicates not significant
* indicates significant at 0.05 level of probability
** indicates significant at 0.01 level of probability

Table 5.26 : Intercorrelations of Family Burden and its Dimensions with the Dependent Variable as Perceived by SOPs

Variable	FB	DRFA	FL	FI	MH	PH	SB	FF
FB	1.000	--	--	--	--	--	--	--
DRFA	0.159†	1.000	--	--	--	--	--	--
FL	0.538**	0.321*	1.000	--	--	--	--	--
FI	0.199†	0.395**	0.350**	1.000	--	--	--	--
MH	0.242†	0.194†	0.285*	0.123†	1.000	--	--	--
PH	0.277*	0.261*	0.542**	0.070†	0.295*	1.000	--	--
SB	0.078†	0.116†	–0.021†	–0.073†	0.253*	0.249†	1.000	--
FF	0.185†	–0.107†	0.327**	0.030†	–0.001†	0.314*	–0.058†	1.000

Note : † indicates not significant
** indicates significant at 0.01 level of probability

on family functioning.

Although the correlation between family burden and the impact of MHC on family functioning was not significant (r=0.188, vide Table 5.26), the above matrix discloses that two components of family burden scale, viz., family leisure and physical health are significantly associated with the impact of MHC on family functioning. The strengths of relationship are about 33 per cent and 31 per cent respectively. Among the other components which did not significantly relate to the impact of MHC on family functioning, are 'disruption in routine family activities', 'mental health' and 'subjective burden' are exhibiting a relationship in negative direction and 'financial burden', 'family interactions' are positively related.

A close examination of the correlation matrix reveals increased burden on physical health and family leisure influenced the impact of MHC on family function as perceived by SOPs. It is a well established fact that increased stress or burden on physical health and reduced leisure time affects the individual's attitudes and performance as reflected in the elevated mean scores of impact of MHC on family functioning.

Section—V

Prediction of Fathers' Perceptions on the Impact of MHC on Family Functioning with their Socio-economic and Family Variables

Step-wise multiple regression analysis, was carried out with the help of 29 independent variables to derive an equation, to predict the impact of MHC on family functioning (FF) and to identify the amount of contribution made by each variable in explaining the variance in the impact of MHC on "Family Functioning". The summary of each step of the multiple regression analysis (which is the output of computer analysis) is given in Table 5.27.

From Table 5.27 it is evident that the first variable that entered into the step-wise multiple regression analysis is Material Possessions (MP). The multiple correlation 'R' is 0.5119 which is nothing but the simple correlation shown in column 11 between family functioning and material possessions (MP) of the father. It can also be observed from the Table that 'R' is significant at 0.01 level

Table 5.27 : Results of Step-Wise Multiple Regression Analysis—Dependent Variable, Family Functioning, Independent Variables, Socio-economic and Family Variables of 'Father'

Step No.	Independent variable entered in each step	Multiple correlation 'R'	R^2	Standard error of multiple correlation	'F' value (d,f) and level of significance	'b' coefficient (or) partial regression coefficient	't' value for 'b' and level of significance	Constant	'B' coefficient	Simple coefficient of correlation with dependent variable	Percentage of variance explained
1	2	3	4	5	6	7	8	9	10	11	12
1.	Material possessions	0.5119	0.2621	15.8343	20.6072** (1,58)	6.5278	4.5395**	122.2845	0.512	0.512	26.2
2.	Behaviour problems	0.6153	0.3786	14.6577	17.3671** (2,57)	6.4857 –6.8003	4.8721** 3.2689**	148.6025	0.509 –0.341	–0.346	26.06 11.80
3.	Size of the Family	0.6732	0.4532	13.8721	15.4728** (3,56)	6.2704 –5.7103 4.1436	4.9675** 2.8439** 2.7638**	123.9735	0.492 –0.287 0.279	0.366	25.19 9.91 10.21
4.	Family Satisfaction	0.7351	0.5404	12.8327	16.1705** (4,55)	5.0564 –5.2157 5.0479 1.6917	4.1222** 2.7985** 3.5679** 3.2310**	78.7438	0.397 –0.262 0.340 0.315	0.388	20.33 9.05 12.44 12.23

Note : † indicates not significant
* indicates significant at 0.05 level of probability
** indicates significant at 0.01 level of probability

(contd.)

Table 5.27 : (contd.)

1	2	3	4	5	6	7	8	9	10	11	12
5.	Marital issues	0.7746	0.6000	12.0824	16.2011**	4.5526	3.8960**	150.3669	0.357	–0.214	18.29
					(5,54)	–6.4956	3.5849**		–0.326		11.28
						3.9251	2.8243**		0.264		9.68
						2.0639	4.0458**		0.385		14.92
						–6.9064	2.8358**		–0.273		5.85
6.	Disruption in routine family activities	0.8040	0.6464	11.4659	16.1524**	4.5610	4.1131**	165.9453	0.358	–0.208	18.32
					(6,53)	–5.9434	3.4312**		–0.298		10.32
						4.8659	3.5617**		0.328		11.99
						1.7579	3.5314**		0.327		12.71
						–7.4715	3.2190**		–0.296		6.32
						–2.7711	2.6388*		–0.239		4.98
7.	Family Type	0.8171	0.6676	11.2238	14.9218**	3.3499	2.6310*	163.0856	0.263	0.400	13.45
					(7,52)	–5.4074	3.1421**		–0.271		9.38
						4.5340	3.3593**		0.305		11.18
						1.9128	3.8669**		–0.356		13.83
						–8.1837	3.5496**		–0.,324		6.91
						–2.7392	2.6642**		–0.237		4.93
						6.4035	1.8197†		0.177		7.07

Note : † indicates not significant
* indicates significant at 0.05 level of probability
** indicates significant at 0.01 level of probability

(F=20.6072 for 1.58 (df). The coefficient of multiple determination (R^2) disclosed that about 26.2 per cent ($R^2 \times 100$) of the variance in the impact of MHC on family functioning is accounted for by material possession alone in the first step. The standard error of multiple estimate (SE of 'R') 15.8343 shown in column 5 revealed that nearly 68 per cent of the obtained scores will be within the range of ±5.8343 points of predicted impact of MHC on family functioning scores.

The partial regression co-efficient (b) presented in column 7 is 6.5278. The 't' value for 'b' (column 8) is significant at 0.01 level. The constant value that will be considered in the equation, at the end of the first step, with which the prediction of family functioning can be made is shown in column 9. The general form of the prediction equation may be given as

$$X^1 = A + b_1 x_1 + b_2 x_2 + b_3 x_3 + \text{........} + b_n x_n$$

where, X^1 denotes the predicted score of dependent variable. 'A' is the constant.

b_1, b_2, b_3 ...., b_n are partial regression coefficients, and x_1, x_2, x_3, ..., x_n are the obtained values on different independent variables.

Thus the actual equation at the end of the first step will be

$$F = 122.2845 + 6.5278 \text{ MP} \qquad (1.1)$$

Behaviour problems of the child as observed by the fathers (BP) entered into the step-wise regression analysis as the second most significant variable. The multiple correlation obtained between the impact of MHC on family functioning on one side and the two independent variables viz., material possession and behaviour problems on the other side is 0.6153. Thus the strength of the relationship between the impact of MHC on family functioning and the two independent variables put together is about 61.53 per cent. The relationship is significant at 0.01 level, the 'F' value 17.367 is far beyond the Table value for 2.57 (d f). The two variables put together can explain about 37.86 per cent (R^2 = 0.3786) of the variance on the impact of MHC on family functioning. Out of this, 26.06 per cent of the variance is explained by material possessions and the remaining 11.80 per cent is accounted by behaviour problems (column 12 of the Table). It is evident that by including behaviour problems, the contribution of material possessions of the father is lowered from 26.2 per cent to 26.06 per cent and this may be due to inter-correlation between the two predictor variables (column 12). These percentages are obtained by multiplying the Beta co-efficients (B – Standard partial coefficients) with the corresponding simple correlations between the dependent variable and the respective independent variable (column 10 and 11 × 100).

The standard error of multiple estimate (SE of R) in column 5 revealed that nearly 68 per cent of the obtained scores on the impact of MHC on family functioning will be within the range of ±14.6577 points of predicted scores of family functioning as perceived by the father of mentally handicapped child. The partial regression coefficients shown in column 7 disclosed, when behaviour problems included as predictor variable, that the impact of MHC on family functioning will increase by 6.8003 points for every unit increase in behaviour problems. Both the partial regression coefficients are significant at 0.01 level as shown in column 8. The regression equation to predict the impact of MHC on family functioning with material possessions and behaviour problems as predictor variables is

$$FF = 148.6025 + 6.4857\ MP - 6.8003\ BP \qquad (1.2)$$

where 148.6025 is the constant to be considered at this step and 6.4857 and –6.8003 are the partial regression coefficients.

In the hierarchy of predictor variables associated with the impact of MHC on family functioning, size of the family (SF) entered as the next important variable. The multiple correlation or the combined association of MP, BP and SF with the impact of MHC on family functioning is 0.6732 which is significant at 0.01 level ($F = 15.4728$ for df 3,56). The value of R^2 (45.32) disclosed that about 45.32 per cent of variance in the impact of MHC on family functioning is explained by these three variables. Out of the variance 25.19 per cent, 9.91 per cent and 10.21 per cent are explained by MP, BP and SF respectively. It is observed that by including size of the family as one more predictor variable, the variance accounted for by MP and BP has gone down from 26.06 per cent to 25.19 per cent and 11.80 per cent to 9.91 per cent due to inter-correlation prevailed among the three independent variables. The standard error of multiple estimate indicate that as many as 68 per cent of the obtained scores on the impact of MHC on family functioning will be within the range of ±13.8721 points of predicted scores of the impact of MHC on family functioning. When these three predictor variables are considered, the partial regression coefficients indicate that the increase on the impact of MHC on family functioning is by 6.2704, –5.7103 and 4.1436 unit for every unit increase in MP, BP and SF respectively. All the three partial regression coefficients are significant at 0.01 level as shown in column 8. The regression equation at this step with constant of 123.9735 will be

$$FF = 123.9735 + 6.2704\ MP - 5.7130\ BP + 4.1436\ SF \tag{1.3}$$

The next variable entered in step-wise regression analysis is family satisfaction (FS). The multiple R is 0.7351 and this is significant beyond 0.01 level. It revealed that the combined strength of relationship between the impact of MHC on family functioning and the related variables viz., MP, BP, SF and FS is 73.51 per cent. All the four predictor variables put together can explain 54.04 per cent (R^2 = 54.04) of the variance on the impact of MHC on family functioning as perceived by the fathers of mentally handicapped children. The variance explained by the variables MP, BP, SF and FS are 20.33 per cent, 9.05 per cent, 12.44 per cent and 12.23 per cent respectively. The equation at this step will be as follows :

$$FF = 78.7436 + 5.0564\ MP - 5.2157\ BP + 5.0479\ SF + 1.6917\ FS \tag{1.4}$$

The next variable that entered into the analysis is marital issues of the father (MI). The multiple 'R' is significant and the strength of the relationship is 77.46 per cent between the impact of MHC on family functioning and host of five predictor variables. All the five variables, viz., MP, BP, SF, FS and MI put together can explain 60.00 per cent of the variance on the impact of MHC on family functioning. The percentage of variance explained by the variables, namely material possession, behaviour problems, size of the family, family satisfaction and marital issues of the father are 18.29, 11.28, 9.68, 14.92 and 5.85 per cent respectively. The individual contributions are obtained by multiplying the Beta coefficients (column 10) with the corresponding simple correlation (column 11) between the predictor variables and the impact of MHC on family functioning as perceived by the father and they are shown in column 12. The partial regression coefficients are significant at 0.01 level. The regression equation can be written with five predictor variables as

$$FF = 150.3669 + 4.5526\ MP - 6.4956\ BP + 3.9251\ SF + 2.0639\ FS - 6.9064\ MI \quad (1.5)$$

The variable that entered into the sixth step is disruption in routine family activities (DRFA). All the six variables put together can explain 64.64 per cent of the variance in the impact of MHC on family functioning as perceived by the father ($R^2 = 0.6464$) and the combined strength of relationship between family function and six predictor variables is 80.40 per cent ($R = 0.8040$). The partial regression coefficients are significant at 0.01 level. The equation with six predictor variables will be

$$FF = 165.9453 + 4.5610\ MP - 5.9434\ BP + 4.8659\ SF + 1.7579\ FS - 7.4715\ MI - 2.7711\ DRFA \quad (1.6)$$

The variable that entered into the seventh step is family type (FT). The multiple 'R' which is significant at 0.01 level is found to be 0.8171. The total variance explained in the dependent variable by the last seven variables is 66.75 per cent i.e., increase of 2.12% only. However the percentage of variance individually explained by the variables MP, BP, SF, FS, MI, DRFA and FT is 13.45, 9.38, 11.18, 13.83, 6.91, 4.93 and 7.07 respectively. But the partial regression coefficients of first six variables are significant at 0.01 level and that of the last was not significant even at 0.05 level. Therefore the equation at the end of the earlier step i.e., Equation 1.6 is the best to predict fathers' perceptions about the impact of MHC on family functioning.

Thus it is evident from Table 5.27 the first six factors, namely, material possession, behaviour problem, size of the family, family satisfaction, marital issues and disruption in routine family activities of the father have turned out to be the significant predictors of the impact of MHC on family functioning as perceived by the father. The 't' values of the partial regression coefficients of these six factors are significant beyond 0.01 level of probability. The remaining 23

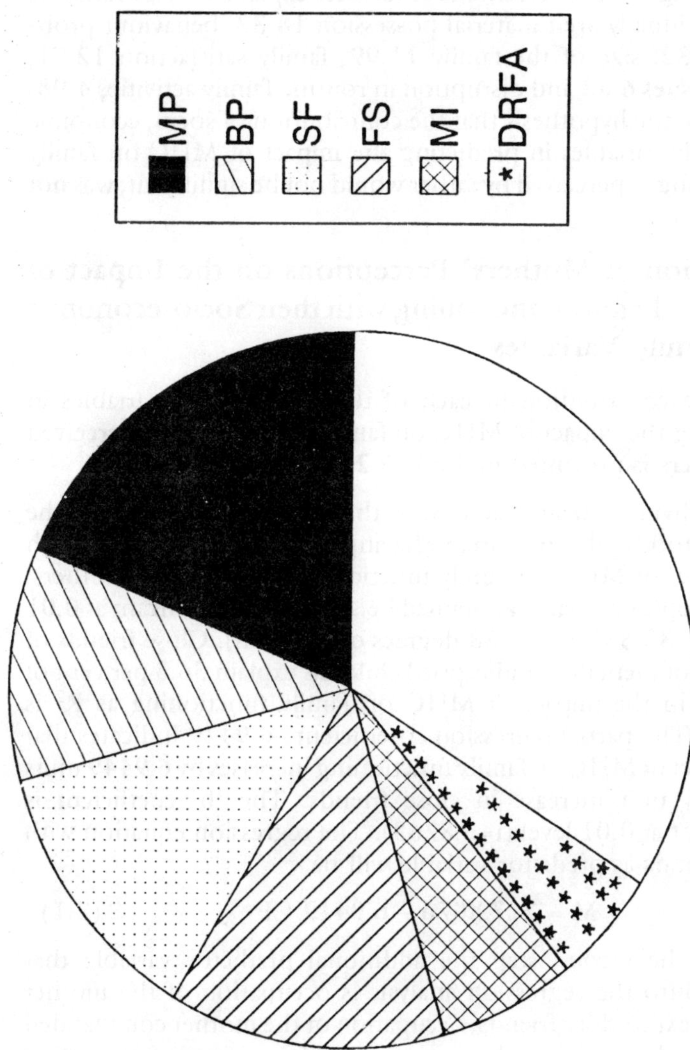

Fig. 5.4 : Percentage Contribution of Independent Variables for the Prediction of Dependent Variable as Perceived by Fathers

variables/dimensions do not contribute to the family functioning significantly as their partial regression coefficients are not significant. The six significant factors put together can explain as much as 64.64 per cent of variance in the impact of MHC on family functioning and the percentage of variance explained by six variables and individually are : material possession 18.32, behaviour problems 10.32, size of the family 11.99, family satisfaction 12.71, marital issues 6.32 and disruption in routine family activities 4.98. Therefore the hypothesis that the contribution of socio, economic and family variables in predicting the impact of MHC on family functioning as perceived by father would not be significant, was not accepted.

Prediction of Mothers' Perceptions on the Impact of MHC on Family Functioning with their Socio-economic and Family Variables

The contribution of each of the 29 predictor variables in predicting the impact of MHC on family functioning as perceived by mothers is presented in Table 5.28 and discussed.

It divulges from Table 5.28 that close friends (CF) of the mother stood as the first variable having very strong association with the impact of MHC on family functioning according to mothers. The multiple correlation obtained i.e., 0.6069 is significant at 0.01 level (F = 33.8356 for 1,58 degrees of freedom). Close friends of mothers of mentally handicapped children explain 36.8 per cent of variance in the impact of MHC on family functioning as R^2 is 0.3684. The partial regression co-efficient –6.9449 indicates that the impact of MHC on family functioning increases by 6.9449 units for every unit increase in close friends. The 'b' coefficient is significant at 0.01 level (t=5.8768). The regression equation with close friends as predictor variable will be

$$M = 217.8076 - 6.9449 \text{ CF} \qquad (2.1)$$

In the second step the additional predictor variable that entered into the regression analysis is occupation of the mother (OC). Next to close friends, occupation of the mother commanded stronger relationship in the impact of MHC on family functioning among the remaining variables. The multiple 'R' is 0.6927 which revealed that the strength of relationship between the dependent

Table 5.28 : Results of Step-Wise Multiple Regression Analysis—Dependent Variable, Family Functioning, Independent Variables, Socio-economic and Family Variables of 'Mother'

Step No.	Independent variable entered in each step	Multiple correlation 'R'	R^2	Standard error of multiple correlation	'F' value (d,f) and level of significance	'b' coefficient (or) partial regression coefficient	't' value for 'b' and level of significance	Constant	'B' coefficient	Simple coefficient of correlation with dependent variable	Percentage of variance explained
1	2	3	4	5	6	7	8	9	10	11	12
1.	Close Friends	0.6069	0.3684	14.0687	33.8356** (1,58)	–6.9449	5.8168**	217.8076	–0.6070	–0.607	36.8
2.	Occupation	0.6927	0.4799	12.8785	26.2972** (2,57)	–5.5305 3.5101	4.7454** 3.4951**	190.6830	–0.4830 0.3560	0.524	29.34 18.65
3.	Marital Issues	0.7249	0.5255	12.4100	20.6746** (3,56)	–5.4915 3.4917 –3.4881	4.8892** 3.6078** 2.3204*	225.6279	–0.4800 0.3540 –0.3050	–0.228	29.13 18.56 6.96
4.	Disruption in routine family activities	0.7529	0.5669	11.9635	17.9996** (4,55)	–5.7256 3.1274 –4.1636 –2.5017	5.2646** 3.3045** 2.8156** 2.2931*	243.8201	–0.5004 0.3172 –0.2550 –0.2106	–0.185	30.38 16.62 5.81 3.89

As the partial regression co-efficients were not significant from the Step-5, further details were not given.

Note : † indicates not significant
* indicates significant at 0.05 level of probability
** indicates significant at 0.01 level of probability

variables and the two independent variables, viz., close friends and occupation is about 69 per cent. The 'F' value obtained is the test for significant of multiple 'R' is 26.2972 for 2,57 degrees of freedom and it is significant beyond 0.01 level. The two variables put together can explain 47.99 per cent of variance in the impact of MHC on family functioning (100 R^2) and out of 47.99 per cent of the variance explained by the two predictor variables, the contribution of close friends is 29.34 per cent and that of occupation is 18.65 per cent. These individual contributions of variables are obtained by calculating the products of Beta coefficient and the corresponding simple correlation co-efficients which are shown in column 10 and 11 in the Table given above and multiplying with 100 (100 R^2). The partial regression coefficients are significant at 0.01 level (column 8), with the constant value 190.683 obtained at this step, the equation will be

$$M = 190.683 - 5.5305\ CF + 3.5101\ OC \qquad (2.2)$$

Marital issues (MI) entered as the next important variable into the regression analysis in step number 3. The combined or cumulated strength of relationship among these three predictor variables and the impact of MHC on family functioning is 72.49 per cent (R= 0.7249). The multiple 'R' is significant at 0.01 level (F=20.6746 for 3,56 degree of freedom). The value of co-efficient of multiple determination R^2 is 0.5255. Therefore, the three variables together can explain 52.55 per cent of variance in the impact of MHC on family functioning. Out of this, the three predictor variables individually contributed 29.13 per cent, 18.56 per cent and 6.96 per cent of the variance in the dependent variable (column 12 of the Table).

The partial regression coefficients at this step reveal that for every unit increase in close friends, occupation and marital issues, the impact of MHC on family functioning will increase by – 5.4915, 3,4917 and –3.4881 units respectively. All the three co-efficients are found to be significant at 0.01 level. The regression equation to predict the impact of MHC on family functioning with three variables can be written as

$$M = 225.6279 - 5.4915\ CF + 3.4917\ OC - 3.4881\ MI \qquad (2.3)$$

The fourth predictor variable that entered into the analysis is disruption in routine family activities (DRFA). The combined strength of relationship among the four variables CF, OC, MI and DRFA and the impact of MHC on family functioning is 75.29 per cent (R=0.7529). The variance explained by all the four predictor variables is 56.69 per cent (R^2=0.5669) and out of this, the contribution made by each variable is, close friends 30.38 per cent, occupation 16.62 per cent, marital issues 5.81 per cent and disruption in routine family activities 3.89 per cent. The equation at this step will be as follows :

$$M = 243.8201 - 5.7256\ CF + 3.1274\ OC - 4.1636\ MI - 2.5017\ DRFA \qquad (2.4)$$

The remaining factors were not shown in the Table because their partial regression coefficients are not significant. Hence it can be concluded that the equation No. 2.4 will be the best equation to predict the impact of MHC on family functioning according to mothers.

The total variance explained by the four variables put together would come to 56.69 per cent, the percentage of variance explained by them individually being 30.38, 16.62, 5.81 and 3.89 respectively. It means that the extent or amount of contribution of these variables to the prediction of the impact of MHC on family functioning as perceived by mothers of mentally handicapped children is different (Fig. 5.5). Therefore, the hypothesis that there would not be any significant variation in the amount of contribution made by different socio-economic and family variables to the prediction of the impact of MHC on family functioning as perceived by mothers of mentally handicapped children is rejected.

Prediction of Significant other Persons' Perceptions on the Impact of MHC on Family Functioning with their Socio-economic and Family Variables

The impact of MHC on family functioning of significant other persons (SOPs) related to mentally handicapped children was predicted with the help of socio-economic and family variables as predictor variables. As above, the step-wise regression analysis was carried out the summary of the computer output is given in Table 5.29 for each step.

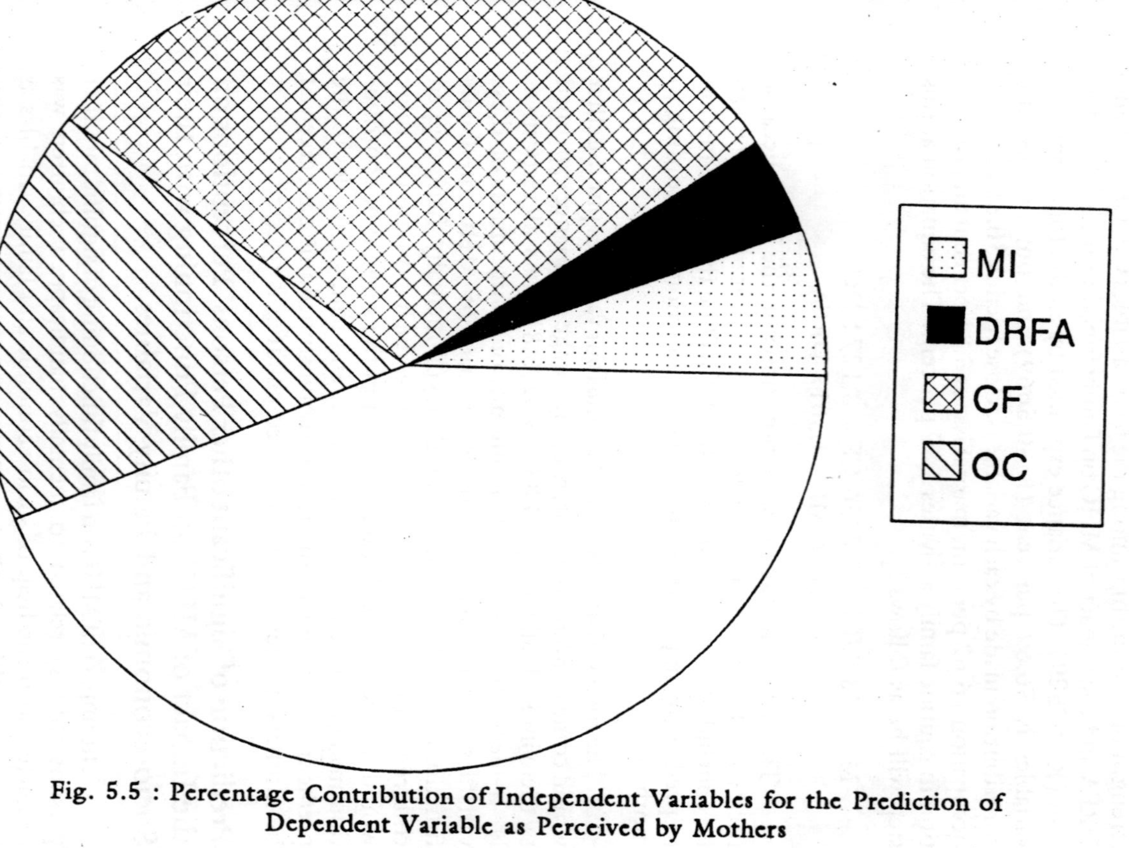

Fig. 5.5 : Percentage Contribution of Independent Variables for the Prediction of Dependent Variable as Perceived by Mothers

Table 5.29 : Results of Step-Wise Multiple Regression Analysis—Dependent Variable, Family Functioning, Independent Variables, Socio-economic and Family Variables of 'SOPs'

Step No.	Independent variable entered in each step	Multiple correlation 'R'	R^2	Standard error of multiple correlation	'F' value (d,f) and level of significance	'b' coefficient (or) partial regression coefficient	't' value for 'b' and level of significance	Constant	'B' coefficient	Simple coefficient of correlation with dependent variable	Percentage of variance explained
1	2	3	4	5	6	7	8	9	10	11	12
1.	Occupation	0.5223	0.2728	13.9154	21.7623** (1,58)	5.1943	4.6650**	124.2148	0.5220	0.522	27.3
2.	Close Friends	0.6327	0.4003	12.7473	19.0251** (2,57)	3.9535	3.6590**	175.0912	0.3980	–0.509	20.76
						–4.3161	3.4809**		–0.3780		19.25
3.	Family Satisfactions	0.6962	0.4847	11.9209	17.5611** (3,56)	3.9823	3.9409**	140.5286	0.4000	0.367	20.90
						–3.7512	3.1940**		–0.3290		16.73
						1.1098	3.0291**		0.2950		10.81
4.	Family leisure	0.7509	0.5639	11.0667	17.7774** (4, 55)	4.2751	4.5352**	112.5500	0.4300	0.367	22.44
						–2.9959	2.6841**		–0.2630		13.36
						1.1418	3.3556**		0.3030		11.12
						3.6180	3.1589**		0.2880		9.42
5.	Community Resources	0.7881	0.6211	10.4101	17.7040** (5,54)	3.5532	3.8536**	121.1735	0.3570	–0.279	18.65
						–2.8891	2.7499**		–0.2530		12.89
						1.1684	3.6488**		0.3100		11.38
						4.5493	4.0416**		0.3620		11.84
						2.6732	2.8561**		–0.2620		7.31

(Contd.)

Table 5.29 (Contd.)

1	2	3	4	5	6	7	8	9	10	11	12
6.	Extended family issues	0.8173	0.6679	9.8366	17.7703**	3.2849	3.7466**	83.4342	0.3300	0.355	17.24
					(6,53)	-2.9028	2.9239**		-0.2540		12.95
						1.0871	3.5756**		0.2890		10.59
						4.2837	4.0108**		0.3410		11.15
						-2.5556	2.8862**		-0.2500		6.98
						2.7233	2.7349**		0.2210		7.83
7.	Behaviour Problems	0.8313	0.6911	9.5788	16.6189**	3.2395	3.7939**	94.8126	0.3260	-0.411	17.00
					(7, 52)	-2.3974	2.3971*		-0.2100		10.69
						0.9891	3.2950**		0.2630		9.64
						3.9137	3.7033**		0.3120		10.19
						-2.5681	2.9783**		-0.2520		7.02
						2.6674	2.7497**		0.2160		7.67
						-2.9239	1.9728†		-0.1670		6.85
8.	Marital Issues	0.8456	0.7151	9.2886	16.0016**	2.7848	3.2504**	77.9092	0.2800	0.438	14.62
					(8, 51)	-1.4097	1.3047†		-0.1240		6.29
						0.9606	3.2963**		0.2550		9.36
						4.0819	3.9707**		0.3250		10.63
						-3.0519	3.5157**		0.3000		8.34
						2.2590	2.3505*		0.2310		8.21
						-3.1017	2.1543*		-0.1780		7.26
						1.8901	2.0735*		0.1450		6.35

9. Family Integration Skills	0.8551	0.7302	9.0399	17.2497**	3.2929	3.9179**	73.2745	0.3310	–0.122	17.28
				(8, 51)	1.1052	3.8421**		0.2930		10.77
					3.8750	3.8517**		0.3080		10.09
					–2.8615	3.3591**		–0.0660		1.86
					2.2806	2.4441**		0.1850		6.56
					–3.6042	2.6606**		0.2050		8.44
					2.2245	2.7767**		0.1700		7.47
					–2.1716	2.1545*		–0.1670		2.03
10. Family Interaction	0.8693	0.7557	8.6870	17.1853**	3.4234	4.2281**	69.5241	0.3440	0.030	17.97
				(9, 50)	1.2038	4.3029**		0.3190		11.71
					3.0881	3.0092*		0.2460		8.04
					–3.1210	3.7764**		–0.3060		8.53
					1.9793	2.1841*		0.2030		7.19
					–3.4361	2.6353*		–0.1960		8.05
					2.8322	3.4774**		0.2170		9.51
					–2.4086	2.4726*		0.2750		3.35
					3.1464	2.2866†		0.1890		0.56
11. Subjective	0.8826	0.7789	8.3471	17.2676**	3.2478	4.1540**	61.4928	0.3266	–0.058	17.06
				(10, 49)	1.1949	4.4447**		0.3172		11.64
					2.8731	2.9003**		0.2288		7.49
					–3.3181	4.1537**		–0.3250		9.07
					2.3768	2.6758**		0.1925		6.84
					–4.3295	3.2970**		–0.2468		10.15
					3.0057	3.8227**		0.3076		13.48
					–2.6782	2.8386*		–0.2056		2.52
					3.4646	2.6058*		0.2085		0.62
					6.9541	2.2705*		0.1677		–0.97

Note : As the partial regression coefficients were not significant from the step 12, the further details were not given.

Note : † indicates not significant * indicates significant at 0.05 level of probability **indicates significant at 0.01 level of probability

In the first step of the analysis, occupation (OC) entered as the most prominent variable. The multiple 'R' 0.5223 is significant at 0.01 level (F=21.7623 for 1,58 degrees of freedom). The coefficient of multiple determination is 0.2728. That means only about 27.28 per cent of the variance in the dependent variable (FF) can be explained by occupation (OC). The equation at the first step will be,

$$SOPs = 124.2148 + 5.1943\ OC \qquad (3.1)$$

Close friends (CF) is the next variable that entered into the analysis. The multiple 'R' 0.6327 is significant at 0.01 level. The total variance that can be explained in the dependent variable, FF, by the two independent variables occupation and close friends is 40.03 per cent, out of which the contribution of OC is 20.76 per cent and the remaining 19.25 per cent is accounted for by close friends of significant other persons related to the mentally handicapped children. The partial regression coefficients for OC and CF are significant at 0.01 level. The constant that should be taken into account is 175.0912 and the prediction equation at the end of this step will be,

$$SOPs = 175.0912 + 3.9535\ OC - 4.3161\ CF \qquad (3.2)$$

Family satisfaction (FS) is the next variable that entered into the analysis. The multiple 'R' increased from 0.6327 to 0.6962. Thus, all the three predictor variable put together can explain only 48.47 per cent of variance in the impact of MHC on family functioning. Whereas the variance explained by three variables individually are : occupation 20.90 per cent, close friends 16.73 per cent and family satisfaction 10.81 per cent. The partial regression coefficients for all the three variables, i.e., OC, CF and FS are highly significant. The prediction equation can be written as;

$$SOPs = 140.5286 + 3.9823\ OC - 3.7512\ CF + 1.1098\ FS \qquad (3.3)$$

The fourth predictor variable that entered into the analysis is family leisure (FL). The combined strength of relationship among the four variables OC, CF, FS and FL and the impact of MHC on family functionig is 75.09 per cent (R=0.7509). The variance that can be explained by all the four predictor variables is 56.39 per cent ($R^2 = 0.5639$). The percentage of variace explained by the variables, namely, occupation, close friends, family satisfaction and family leisure are 22.44, 13.36, 11.12 and 9.42 respectively. The contribution of each variable, the standard error of multiple estimate, the level of significance and the partial regression coefficients of all the variables are significant at 0.01 level. The equation at this step will be as follows;

$$SOPs=112.55+4.2751\ OC-2.9959\ CF+1.1418\ FS+3.6180\ FL \quad (3.4)$$

Community resources (CR) is the next significant predictor variable in the analysis. The multiple 'R' which is significant at 0.01 level, is found to be 0.7881. The total variance that can be explained in the impact of MHC on family functioning by the host of five variables is 62.11 per cent. The variance explained by the variables occupation, close friends, family satisfaction, family leisure, and community resources of the significant other persons related to the mentally handicapped children are 18.65, 12.89, 11.38, 11.84 and 7.31 per cent respectively. All the partial regression coefficients are found to be significant at 0.01 level. The equation at this step of the analysis can be written as;

$$SOPs = 121.1735 + 3.5532\ OC - 2.8891\ CF + 1.1684\ FS + 4.5493\ FL - 2.6732\ CR \quad (3.5)$$

The sixth predictor variable that entered into the analysis is extended family issues (EFI). The combined strength of relationship between the six variables —OC, CF, FS, FL CR and EFI and the impact of MHC on family functioning is 81.73 per cent (R = 0.8173). The variance explained by all six predictor variables is 66.79 per cent ($R^2 = 0.6679$) and out of this, the contribution made by each variable is occupation 17.24, close friends 12.95 per cent, family satisfaction 10.59 per cent, family leisure 11.15 per cent, community resources 6.98 per cent extended family issues 7.83 per cent. The equation at this step will be as follows :

$$SOPs = 83.4342 + 3.2849\ OC - 2.9028\ CF + 1.0871\ FS + 4.2837\ FL - 2.5556\ CR + 2.7233\ EFI \quad (3.6)$$

Behaviour problems (BP) is the next significant predictor variable in the analysis. The multiple 'R' which is significant at 0.01 level, is found to be 0.8313. The total variance that can be explained in the impact of MHC on family functioning by the host seven variables is 69.11 per cent. The variance explained by the variables occupation, close friends, family satisfaction, family leisure, community resources, extended family issues and behaviour problems are 17.00, 10.69, 9.64, 10.19, 7.02, 7.67 and 6.85 per cent respectively. All the partial regression coefficients are found to be significant at 0.05 level. The equation at this step of the analysis can be written as;

$$\text{SOPs} = 94.8126 + 3.2395\ \text{OC} - 2.3974\ \text{CF} + 0.9891\ \text{FS} + 3.9137\ \text{FL} - 2.5681\ \text{CR} + 2.6674\ \text{EFI} - 2.9239\ \text{BP} \qquad (3.7)$$

The variable that entered into the eighth step is the marital issues (MI). All the eight variables put together can explain 71.52 per cent of variance in the impact of MHC on family functioning of significant to the person related to mentally handicapped children (R^2=0.7151) and the combined strength of eight predictor variables is 84.56 per cent (R = 0.8456). The variance explained by eight variables individually are; occupation 14.62 per cent, close friends 6.29 per cent, family satisfaction 9.36 per cent, family leisure 10.63 per cent, community resources 8.34 per cent, extended family issues 8.21 per cent, behaviour problems 7.26 per cent and marital issues 6.35 per cent. The prediction equation at this step with the constant value and the partial regression coefficient shown in column 9 and 7 respectively will be;

$$\text{SOPs} = 77.9092 + 2.7848\ \text{OC} - 1.4097\ \text{CF} + 0.9606\ \text{FS} + 4.0819\ \text{FL} - 3.0519\ \text{CR} + 2.2590\ \text{EFI} - 3.1017\ \text{BP} + 1.8901\ \text{MI} \qquad (3.8)$$

The obtained 't' value (Table 5.29) of the partial regression coefficients of the factors except the variable close friends the remaining variables viz., occupation, family satisfaction, family leisure, community resources, extended family issues, behaviour problems and marital issues are significant.

In the hierarchy of predictor variables associated with the impact of MHC on family functioning of significant other persons related to mentally handicapped children, family integration skills (FIS) entered as the next important variable. The multiple correlation or the combined association of OC, FS, FL, CR, EFI, BP,

MI and FIS with family function is 0.8551 which is significant at 0.01 level (F=17.2497 for 8,51 degrees of freedom). The value of R^2 (0.7302) disclosed that about 73.02 per cent of the variance in the impact of MHC on family functioning is explained by these variables. Out of this variance 17.28, 10.77, 10.09, 1.86, 6.56, 8.44, 7.47 and 2.03 per cents are explained by OC, FS, FL, CR, EFI, BP, MI and FIS respectively. All the partial regression coefficients are significant at 0.05 level as shown in column 8. The regression equation at this step with the constant of 73.2745 will be;

$$\text{SOPs} = 73.2745 + 3.2929\ \text{OC} + 1.1052\ \text{FS} + 3.8750\ \text{FL} - 2.8615\ \text{CR} + 2.2806\ \text{EFI} - 3.6042\ \text{BP} + 2.2245\ \text{MI} - 2.1716\ \text{FIS} \quad (3.9)$$

The next variable entered into the step-wise regression analysis is family interaction (FI). The multiple 'R' is 0.8693 and this is significant beyond 0.01 level. It revealed that the combined strength of relationship between the impact of MHC on family functioning and the related variables, viz., OC, FS, FL, CR, EFI, BP, MI, FIS and FI is 87 per cent. Thus the increase in the 'R' is 2.0 per cent only.

All the nine predictor variables put together can explain 75.57 per cent (R^2 = 0.7557) of the variance in the impact of MHC on family functioning of significant other persons related to mentally handicapped children. The partial regression coefficients are significant at 0.05 level. The equation with nine predictor variables will be;

$$\text{SOPs} = 69.5241 + 3.4234\ \text{OC} + 1.2038\ \text{FS} + 3.0881\ \text{FL} - 3.1210\ \text{CR} + 1.9793\ \text{EFI} - 3.4361\ \text{BP} + 2.8322\ \text{MI} - 2.4086\ \text{FIS} + 3.1464\ \text{FI} \quad (3.10)$$

Subjective burden (SB) is the next most significant predictor variable in the analysis. The multiple 'R' which is significant at 0.01 level is found to be 0.8826. The total variance explained in the dependent variable by the host of ten variables is 77.89 per cent. The percentage of variance explained individually by the variable occupation, family satisfaction, family leisure, community resources, extended family issues, behaviour problems, marital issues,

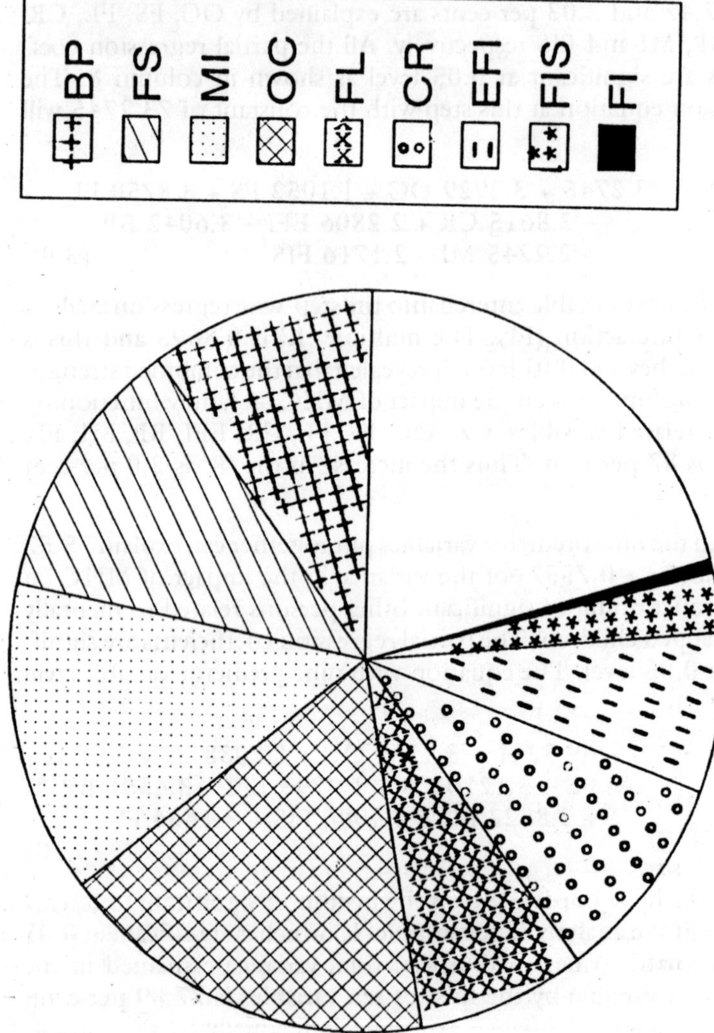

Fig. 5.6 : Percentage Contribution on Independent Variables for the Prediction of Dependent variable as Perceived by SOPs

family integration skills, family interaction and subjective burden is 17.06, 11.64, 7.49, 9.07, 6.84, 10.15, 13.48, 2.52, 0.62 and 0.97 respectively. The partial regression coefficients are significant at 0.05 level or at 0.01 level. The regression equation can be written with ten predictor variables as;

$$\begin{aligned} \text{SOPs} = 61.4928 &+ 3.2478 \text{ OC} + 1.1949 \text{ FS} + 2.8731 \text{ FL} \\ &- 3.3181 \text{ CR} + 2.3768 \text{ EFI} - 4.3295 \text{ BP} \\ &+ 3.0057 \text{ MI} - 2.6782 \text{ FIS} + 3.4646 \text{ FI} \\ &+ 6.9541 \text{ SB} \end{aligned} \qquad (3.11)$$

Thus the total variance explained by eleven variables put together would come to 77.89 per cent. It means that the extent or amount of contribution of these variables to the prediction of the impact of MHC on family functioning as perceived by significant other persons related to MHC is different (Fig. 5.6). Hence, the hypothesis that, the contribution of socio-economic and family variables in predicting the impact of MHC on family functioning as perceived by significant other persons would not vary significantly; is rejected.

An important trend which has emerged from the study is the differential pattern of contribution by the independent variables to the dependent variable. Difference is seen in the perceptions of three groups respondents with regard to the percentage of contribution of independent variables in predicting the dependent variable. Fathers perceived that material possessions, behaviour problems, size of the family satisfaction, marital issues, disruption in routine family activities and family type as the variables which could predict the impact of MHC on family functioning. The contribution of all the above mentioned variables put together amounted to 64.64% of variance, whereas for mothers fewer variables entered into the regression analysis. They are close friends, occupation, marital issues and disruption in routine family activities. All these four variables put together contributed 56.70 per cent of variance. It is interesting to note that in the case of fathers two independent variables with a single score namely behaviour problems and family satisfaction entered into the regression analysis. The remaining variables which entered were dimensions of SES, resources and burden scale, whereas in the case of mothers all the variables entered into the regression analysis were only dimensions of SES, resources

Table 5.30 : Significant Socio-economic and Family Variables for Predicting the Impact of MHC on Family Functioning According to Three Groups of Respondents

Sl.No.	*Variables*	*Fathers*	*Mothers*	*SOPs*
1.	Material possessions	18.32	--	--
2.	Behaviour Problems	10.32	--	10.15
3.	Size of the Family	11.99	--	--
4.	Family Satisfaction	12.71	--	11.64
5.	Marital Issues	6.32	5.81	13.48
6.	Disruption in Routine Family Activities	4.98	3.89	--
7.	Family Type	--	--	--
8.	Close Friends	--	30.38	--
9.	Occupation	--	16.62	17.06
10.	Family Leisure	--	--	7.49
11.	Community Resources	--	--	9.07
12.	Extended Family Issues	--	--	6.84
13.	Family Integration Skills	--	--	2.52
14.	Family Interaction	--	--	0.62
15.	Subjective Burden	--	--	–0.97

and burden scale.

With regard to SOPs perceptions, 77.90 per cent of variance was explained by a bunch of ten variables/dimensions viz., occupation, family satisfaction, family leisure, community resources, extended family issues, behaviour problems, marital issues, family integration skills, family interaction and subjective burden.

Our last hypothesis, that the impact of MHC on family functioning cannot be predicted with the help of independent variables as perceived by fathers, mothers and SOPs is not accepted as revealed by the results, illustrated in Figures 4, 5 and 6.

To conclude as Miles (1992) had recommended that there are some basic steps a family can take such as re-orienting their own attitudes towards their handicapped child and some simple behavioural techniques that can help parents to manage difficult behaviour and help the child to learn what is acceptable. In view of the stress experienced by families, a dire need is there to devise methods of intervention which addresses the issue of stress in the family. The interventions should be geared towards reduction of stress and improvement of family adaptation. This can be achieved by increasing the child's competence through home based individual training. In this connection it is worth mentioning Krishnaswamy's (1992) words "Our country cannot have a million professionals to give individual training to a million children, but we do have a million mothers to given individual training to their children." Inspite of the fact that India is not a well developed country, the country has a number of rich cultural factors which are conducive for better integration and easy normalization of MHC. Such of those factors are :

- Family's interest and concern in the child.
- Warmth and affection shown by the extended family members.
- lose kinship relationships (especially in rural areas).
- Utmost importance given by family members to family obligations and loyalties especially in times of crisis.
- Help and assistance rendered by the neighbours especially typical of rural areas.

Keeping all the above factors in mind intervention programmes can be planned to help families with MHC to alleviate the stressful effects by utilizing the family strengths in providing quality care to MHC.

Major Findings of the Study

1. Majority of the families had male mentally handicapped children. Nearly half of the children are first borns. One third of the children belonged to childhood, late childhood and adolescent groups each.
2. Consanguineous marriages were very common in families of MHC.

3. Majority of the respondents were Hindus.
4. Nearly half of the families of study belonged to nuclear type whereas one third of them were joint type and the remaining families were extended type.
5. Nearly two thirds of the families studied, had one to three children and remaining one third had four and more than four children.
6. Nearly half of the families were small in size having three to six members and the remaining families had seven and more than seven members.
7. Mostly grandparents had fallen into the category of significant other persons. Siblings came next, followed by aunts and uncles; Grandparents, aunts and uncles mostly belonged to paternal side.
8. Fathers, mothers and significant other persons perceived the impact of MHC on family functioning to a great extent.
9. The three groups of respondents differed significantly in their perceptions about personal health, marital issues, extended family support, personal resources, marital resources, and family coping skills.
10. Socio-economic status had a high and significant positive correlation with the impact of MHC on family functioning for the three groups of respondents.
11. Family resources as a whole did not influence the impact of MHC on family functioning as perceived by fathers.
12. Mothers (and SOPs) perceived that family resources can dilute the impact of MHC on family functioning.
13. Only fathers perceived that family coping skills can reduce the impact of MHC on family functioning.
14. Close friends were considered to be important in lessening the impact of MHC on family functioning by mothers and SOPs but not by fathers.

15. Family integration was not perceived as a significant variable in influencing the impact of MHC on family functioning by all.

16. Perception of fathers and mothers about family burden did not significantly influence the impact of MHC on family functioning. Whereas SOPs perceived that two dimensions of family burden scale viz., family leisure and physical health could influence significantly the impact of MHC on family functioning.

17. Family satisfaction was significantly and positively associated with the impact of MHC on family functioning as viewed by the three groups of respondents.

18. Behaviour problems were perceived by fathers as significantly influencing the impact of MHC on family functioning whereas mothers did not perceive such a relationship. SOPs viewed a negative relationship between behaviour problems and the impact of MHC on family functioning.

19. Fathers perceived that material possessions, behaviour problems, size of the family, family satisfaction, marital issues, disruption in routine family activities and family type were the significant predictors of the impact of MHC on family functioning. The contribution of all the above mentioned variables put together amounted to 66.64 per cent of variance in the dependent variable.

20. Only four variables viz., Close friends, Occupation, Marital issues and Disruption in routine family activities entered into the regression analysis for mothers. All the four variables put together contributed 56.70 per cent of the variance in the dependent variable.

21. The percentage of variance explained by ten different variables was 77.90 per cent for SOPs. They are occupation, family satisfaction, family leisure, community resources, extended family issues, behaviour problems, marital issues, family integration skills, family interaction and subjective burden.

Implications

The implications of the present research are that the knowledge of the perceptual differences of family members (fathers, mothers and SOPs) about the stressful effects on family with a mentally handicapped child may assist interventionists in planning social support programmes for such families.

Identification of various factors which protect families from the stress of caring for mentally handicapped children will enable professionals and service providers in rendering efficient family support.

Families with mentally handicapped children can be helped to utilize family strengths in providing quality care for the handicapped children.

The results of the present study may be helpful in developing comprehensive models of family based interventions which is a dire necessity in the Indian context especially for rural areas. Individual family goals, energies, their living styles and family philosophy need to be considered in planning intervention programmes.

The results of the present study may be helpful in planning effective intervention programmes to lessen family stress with a mentally handicapped child through capitalizing on the family strengths and by increasing child's competence. Behaviour modification techniques can be included in the pool of intervention services.

Limitations

The following are the limitations or constraints experienced during the course of the present investigation.

1. A small sample was taken up due to the nature of the problem and time constraint.
2. Generalization could not be made owing to the size of the sample.
3. The severity in the handicappedness was not taken into consideration as this study was concerned about the stressful effects on family as perceived by three groups of respondents.

Suggestions for Further Research

The following are the suggestions for further research which will enable for thorough understanding of the problem.

1. A longitudinal study of perceptions of different family members over a time frame of 5 years may be taken up, if we are to draw generalized conclusions.
2. The effect of need-based and home-based intervention programmes for families may be studied.
3. Family interaction patterns in the families with mentally handicapped child may be studied.

Summary

Raising a mentally handicapped child in a family involves many difficulties and problems to the parents and other family members. Because of these difficulties and problems the family functioning in such families gets affected. So the main objective of the present study is to understand the stressful effects on the family in rearing and managing a mentally handicapped child.

The following were the hypothesis formulated for empirical verification.

Hypotheses

1. Fathers, mothers and significant other persons differ significantly in their perceptions about stressful effects on the family in rearing and managing a mentally handicapped child.

2. Socio-demographic variables significantly influence the family functioning in families with a mentally handicapped child.

3. Family variables like type and size of the family, family resources and family satisfaction, significantly influence the family functioning in families with a mentally handicapped child.

4. The perceptions of family members about the burden of raising a mentally handicapped child significantly influence the family functioning.

5. Behaviour problems exhibited by the mentally handicapped child significantly influence the family functioning.

6. The impact of mentally handicapped child on family functioning cannot be predicted with the help of independent variables as perceived by fathers, mothers and significant other persons.

A rural screening camp was conducted in the year 1989 in Chandragiri Mandal of Chittoor District (Andhra Pradesh) by Thakur Hariprasad Institute of Research and Rehabilitation for the Mentally Handicapped in collaboration with Bala Sevika Training Institute, Tirupati for which the present investigator was then working as Principal. Out of one hundred and forty six (146) children who were identified in a door to door survey, only one hundred and seventeen (117) children attended the screening camp. The remaining twenty nine (29) children were dropouts. Seventy children (70) were included in the sample who satisfied the inclusion criteria from those who attended the camp.

The present study was conducted in two stages viz., pilot study and final study. Pilot study was conducted on a sample of ten families of these mentally handicapped children for the purpose of evaluation of major tools and the procedure to be finally employed. Remaining sixty (60) children's families were included in the final study for the purpose of collecting primary data on all major tools. Fathers, mothers and significant other persons in the family were the respondents for the study.

After careful scrutiny of the relevant literature available a need was felt for the development of culture relevant tools for the study of family resources, family coping, family integration and family functioning. Following were the four tools developed by the investigator for data collection.

1. Family Resources Scale (FRS)
2. Family Coping Scale (FCS)
3. Family Integration Scale (FIS)
4. Family Functioning Scale (FFS)

The following four tools which were available are also used for collection of information on SES, family burden, family satisfaction and behaviour problems in mentally handicapped children.

1. Socio-Economic Status Scale (Rural) (Trivedi and Uday Pareek, 1964).

2. Family Burden Scale (FBS) (Pai and Kapur, 1981)
3. Family Satisfaction Scale (FSS) (Smilkstein, 1978)
4. Behaviour Problem Checklist (PBCL) (Peshawaria et al., 1990)

Necessary information was collected using all the eight tools mentioned earlier from fathers, mothers and significant other persons in the family. Different tools were administered in two sessions. The data thus collected was scored, means and SDs were calculated and then subjected to suitable statistical techniques.

The salient findings are summed up in the following paragraph bearing in mind the objective, hypotheses and methodological limitations.

1. SES significantly influenced the impact of MHC on family functioning.
2. Fathers, mothers and significant other persons differed significantly in their perceptions about personal health, marital issues, extended family support, personal resources, marital resources and family coping skills.
3. The three groups of respondents did not differ in their perceptions about burden of raising a MHC except in one dimension i.e., disruption in routine family activities.
4. The three groups of respondents perceived the impact of MHC on family functioning at the same level.
5. The extent of correlation among different variables is different for the three groups of respondents.
6. The percentage of contribution explained by independent variables in the prediction of dependent variable differed for three groups of respondents.

Studies of this nature are of great help in planning intervention programmes and need based parent education programmes. The policy makers can also make use of the results of the present study while developing family support systems.

Bibliography

Abidin, R.R. and Burk, W.T. (1978). Parenting stress index. Unpublished Manuscripts. Department of Foundations of Education, University of Virginia.

Adams, M.E. (1968). Problems in management of mentally retarded children with cerebral palsy. *The Cerebral Palsy Journal.*

Agathonos, H. and Vales, T. (1982). Families of children with Down's Syndrome in Greece. *Journal of Comparative Studies*, Vol. XIII, No. 2, 221–229.

Akerley, M. (1975). The invulnerable parent. *Journal of Autism and Childhood Schizophrenia*, 5, 275–281.

Alvey, G.L. and Aeschleman, S.R. (1990). Evaluation of parent training programme for teaching mentally retarded children. Age–Appropriate Restaurant Skills: a preliminary investigation. *Journal of Mental Deficiency Research*, 34, 421–428.

Baker, B.L., Landen, S.J. and Kashina, K.J. (1991). Effects of parent training on families of children with mental retardation; Increased Burden or Generalised Benefit. American *Journal on Mental Retardation*, Vol. 96, No. 2, 127–136.

Balachandran, R. (1985). The role of a family in the promotion of mental health of one of it's members : A case study. *The Indian Journal of Social Work*, Vol. XLV, No. 4, 403–413.

Barkley, R.A. (1981). Hyperactivity in E.J. Mash and L.G. Terdal (Ed.) *Behavioural Assessment of Childhood Disorders.* Newyork

: Guilford Press.

Baxter, C. (1992). Appraised significance of intellectual disability for parents of children in three age cohorts : Exploring the stress process. *Journal of Intellectual Disability Research*, 36, 519–529.

Beckman, P.J. and Bell, P. (1981). Child related stress in families of handicapped children. Topics in Early Childhood Special Education, 1(3), 45–54.

Beckman, P.J. (1983). Influence of selected child characteristics on stress in families of handicapped infants. *American Journal of Mental Deficiency*, Vol. 88, No. 2, 150–156.

Beckman, P.J. (1991). Comparison of mother's and father's perceptions of the effect of young children with and without disabilities. *American Journal on Mental Retardation*, Vol. 95, No. 5, 585–595.

Begab, M.J. and Richardson, S.A. (1975). *The mentally retarded and society : A social science perspective*, London : London University Press.

Bernsen, A.H. (1976). Severe mental retardation among children in the country of Aarhus, Denmark, *Acta Psychiat Scand*, 54, 43–66.

Bernsen, A.H. (1981). Children's handicaps, behaviour and skills schedule (HBS) rating scale results. *Acta Psychiat Scand Suppt*, 285, Vol. 62, 249–257.

Bhat, V.K. and Gauba, S. (1978). A marital adjustment questionnaire in Hindi. *Indian Journal of Clinical Psychology*, 5, 29–32.

Bhatti, R.S. and Narayan, H.S. (1980). Parental attitude questionnaire, unpublished manuscript, Bangalore. National Institute of Mental Health and Neuro Sciences.

Biswas, M. "Mentally retarded and normal children". Sterling Publishers Pvt. Ltd.

Black M.M., Molaison, V.A. and Smull, M.W. (1990). Families caring for a young adult with mental retardation : service needs and urgency of community living requests. *Americal Journal on Mental Retardation*, Vol. 95, No. 1, 32–39.

Boss, P. (1988). Family Stress Management. Sage Publications, India.

Bradshaw, J. and Lawton, D. (1978). Tracing the Causes of stress in families with handicapped children. *British Journal of Social Work*, 8 (2), 181–191.

Breiner, J. and Forehand, R. (1982). Mother-child interaction : A comparison of clinic referred developmentally delayed group and two non-delayed groups. Applied Research in Mental Retardation, 3, 175–183.

Brinkworth, R. (1970). The reaction of parents to the diagnosis of sub-normality Unpublished paper.

Bristol, M. Schopler, E. and McConnanghey, R. (1984). Prevalence of separation and divorce in unserved families of young autistic and autistic–like children. Paper presented at the annual Handicapped Children's Early Education Programmes Conference, Washington, D.C.

Bristol, M. Gallagher, J.J. and Schopler, E. (1988). Mothers and fathers of young developmentally disabled and non-disabled boys : Adaptation and spousal support. *Developmental Psychology*, 24, 441–451.

Brody, G.H. Stoneman, Z., Crapps, M.J. and Davis, C.H. (1991). Observations of the role relations and behaviour between older children with mental retardation and their younger siblings. *American Journal on Mental Retardation*, Vol. 95, Nov. 5, 527–536.

Bromley, B.E. and Blacher, J. (1991). Parental reasons for out-of-home placement of children with severe handicaps. *Mental Retardation*, Vol. 29, No. 5, 275–280.

Bronfenbrenner, U. (1977). Toward an experimental ecology of human development. *American Psycholgists*, 32, 513–531.

Brotherson, M.J. Houghton, J. Turnbull, A.P., Bronicki, G.J., Gordon, C.R., Summers, J.A. and Turnbull, H.R. (1988). Education and trainging in mental retardation–September, 165–172.

Burr, W.R. (1973). Family under stress. Theory construction and sociology of the family, 199–217. A Wiley Interscience Publication : John Wiley & Sons.

Butler, N., Gill, R., Pomeroy, D. and Fartrell, J. (1978). Handicapped children–their homes and life styles. Department of Child Health, University of Bristol.

Byrne, E.A. and Cunningham, C.C. (1985). The effects of mentally handicapped children on familiesùA conceptual review. *Journal of Child Psychology and Psychiatry*, Vol. 26, No. 6, 847–864.

Caldwell, B.M. and Gaze, S.B. (1960). *American Journal of Mental Deficiency*, 64, 845.

Caplan, G. (1976). The family as support system in support systems and mutual help by G. Caplan and M. Killiea (Eds). New York : Gru'ne & Stratton.

Carver, J. and Carver, N. (1972). *The family of the retarded child. Syracuse*, New York : Syracuse University Press.

Cole, D.A.(1986). Out-of-home child placement and family adaptation : A theoretical frame work. *American Journal of Mental Deficiency*, 91, 226–236.

Cole, D.A. and Meyer, L.H. (1989). Impact of needs and resources on family plans to seek out-of-home placement. *American Journal on Mental Retardation*, Vol. 93, No. 4, 380–387.

Crnic, K.A., Friedrich, W.N. and Greenberg, M.T. (1983). Adaption of families with mentally retarded children. A model of stress coping and family ecology. *American Journal of Mental Deficiency*, Vol. 88, No. 2, 125–138.

Crnic, K.A. and Greenber, M.T. (1990). Minor parenting stresses with young children. *Child Development*, 61, 1628–1637.

Cullen, J.C., Maclead, J.A., Williams, P.D. and Williams, A.R. (1992). Coping satisfaction and the life cycle in families with mentally retarded persons. Issues in comprehensive *Paediatric Nursing*, Vol. 14, No. 3, 193–207.

Cummings, S.T. Bayley, H.C. and Rie, H.E. (1966). Effects of the child's deficiency on the mother'A study of mothers of mentally retarded chronically ill and neurotic children. *American Journal of Orthopsychiatry* 36, 595.

Cummings, S.T. (1976). The impact of the child's deficiency on the father : A study of fathers on mentally retarded and chronically ill children. *American Journal of Orthopsychiatry*, 46, 246–258.

Cunningham, C.E., Rueler, E. and Blackwell, J. (1981). Behavioural and linguistic developments in the interactions of normal and retarded children with their mothers. *Child Development*, 52, 62–70.

Darling, R.B. (1979). Families against society. Sage Beverly Hill, C.A.

Davis, D. (1967). Family processes in mental retardation. American *Journal of Psychiatry*, 124 : 3, 340–350.

Davis, H. and Rushton, R. (1991). Counselling and supporting parents of children with developmental delay : A research evaluation. *Journal of Mental Deficiency Research*, 35, 89–112.

Davis, M. and Mackay, D. (1973). Mentally subnormal children and their families. The Lancet, Oct., 27, 5.

Delvecchio Good, M.J. (1979). The familiear AGPAR index : A study construct validity. *The Journal of Family Practice*, 8, (No. 3), 577–582.

DeMayer, M.D. (1979). Parents and children in stress. Washington, D.C. : Winston.

Deykin, E.Y. (1972). Life functioning in families of delinquent boys : An assessment model. *Social Service Review*, 46, (No. 7), 90–103.

Donovan, A.M. (1988). Family stress and ways of coping with adolescents who have handicaps : Maternal perceptions. *American Journal on Mental Retardation*, Vol. 92, No. 6, 502–509.

Dunst, C.J., Trivette, C.M. and Cross, A.H. (1988). Mediating Influences of Social Support : Personal, Family and Child outcomes. *American Journal of Mental Deficiency*, Vol. 90, No. 4, 403–417.

Dupont, A. (1980). A study concerning the time-related and other burdens when severely handicapped children are reared at home. *Acta Psychiat Scand Suppt*, 285, Vol. 62, 249–257.

Dupont, A. (1986). Socio-psychiatric aspects of the young severely, mentally retarded and the family. *British Journal of Psychiatry*, 148, 227–234.

Dutta, B. (1985). Appraisal of psychological behavioural problems of school children. Presented at 7th World Congress of IAASMR, New Delhi.

Dybwad, G. (1982). The rediscovery of the family. *Mental Retardation*, Vol. 32, No. 1, 18–31.

Dyson, L.L. (1991). Families of young children with handicaps : parental stress and family functioning. *American Journal on Mental Retardation*, Vol. 95, No. 6, 623–629.

Dyson, L.L. (1993). Response to the presence of a child with disabilities : Parental stress and family functioning over time. *American Journal on Mental Retardation*, Vol. 98, No. 2, 207–218.

Erickson, M. and Upshur, C.C. (1989). Care taking burden and social support, comparison of mothers of infants with an without disabilities. *American Journal on Mental Retardation*, Vol. 94, No. 3, 250–258.

Eyman, R.K. and Call, T. (1977). Maladaptive behaviour and community placement of mentally retarded persons. *American Journal of Mental Deficiency*, 82.2, 137–144.

Farber, B. (1959). Effects of a severely mentally retarded child on family integration. Monographs of the Society for Research in Child Development, 24 (2 Serial No. 71).

Farber, B. (1960). Perception of crisis and related variables in the impact of retarded child in the mother. *Journal of Health and Human Behaviour*, 1 (2, 108–118).

Farber, B. and Ryckman, D. (1965). Effects of severely Mentally Retarded children and Family Relationships. *Mental Retardation Abstract*, 2 (1, 1–17).

Farber, B. (1975). Family adaptations to severely mentally retarded children. in B. Begab and Richardson (Eds). The mentally retarded and society : social science perspective. Baltimore University : Park Press.

Farber, B. Rowtiz, L. (1986). Families with a mentally retarded child. In N.F. Ellis and N.W. Bray (Eds.), International review of Research in Mental Retardation, Vol. 14, 201–222. New York : Academic Press.

Fatheringham John, B., Kelton, Mora, Hoddinott and Bernard, A. (1971). Retarded child and his family : Effects of home and institution. Monograph Series II, Ontario.

Featherstone, H. (1980). A difference in the family living with a disabled child. New York : Penguin Books.

Ferguson, N. and Watt, J. (1980). The mothers of children with special educational needs. *Scottish Educational Review*, 12, 21–31.

Fisher, B.L., Giblin, P.R. and Hoopes, M.H. (1982). Healthy family functioning : What therapists say and what families want? *Family Studies Review Year Book*, 563–575.

Floyd, F.J. and Phillippe, K.A. (1993). Parental interactions with children with and without mental retardation : Behaviour management, coerciveness and positive exchange. *American Journal of Mental Retardation*, Vol. 97, No. 6, 673–684.

Flynt, S.W. and Wood, T.A. (1989). Stress and coping of mothers of children with moderate mental retardation. *American Journal on Mental Retardation*, Vol. 94, No. 3, 278–283.

Flynt, S.W., Wood, T.A. and Scott, R.L. (1992). Social Support of Mothers of Children with Mental Retardation. *Mental Retardation*, Vol. 30, No. 4, 233–236.

Folkman, S., Shaefer, C. and Lazarus, R.S. (1979). Cognitive processes as mediators of stress and coping. M.V. Hamilton and D.W. Warburton (Eds). *Human Stress and Cognition*, (206–298). New York: John Wiley.

Frey, K.S., Greenberg, M.T. and Fewell, R.R. (1989). Stress and coping among parents of handicapped children : A Multi-

Dimensional Approach, Vol. 94, No. 3, 240–249.

Friedrich, W.N. (1979). Predictors of the coping Behaviour of Mothers of Handicapped Children. *Journal of Consulting and Clinical Psychology*, 47, 1140–1141.

Friedrich, W.N. and Friedrich, W.L. (1981). Psycho-social assets of parents of handicapped and non-handicapped children. *American Journal of Mental deficiency*, 85, 551–553.

Friedrich, W.N. Greenber, M.T. and Crnic, K. (1983).A Short form of the questionnaire on resources and stress. *American Journal of Mental Deficiency*, Vol. 88, No. 1, 41–48.

Friedrich, W.N., Greenber, M.T. and Crnic, K. (1985). The effects of developmental disabilities on children and families : Measurement issues and conceptual frameworks. Effects on families, 357–375.

Friedrich, W.N., Wilturner, L.T. and Cohen, D.S. (1985). Coping resources and parenting mentally retarded children. *American Journal of Mental Deficiency*, Vol. 90, No. 2, 130–139.

Gallagher, J., Beckman, P. and Cross, A. (1983). Families of handicapped children : Sources of stress and its amelioration. *Exceptional children*, 50, 10–19.

Gandotra, V.S. (1985). Management problems and practices of home makers with a disabled member in the family. *The Indian Journal of Social Work*, Vol. XLV, No. 4, 485–490.

Garett H.E. and Wood Worth R.S. (1981). Statistics in psychology and education, Vakils, pfeffer and Simons Ltd., Bombay.

Gath, A. (1974). Sibling reactions to mental handicap : A comparison of the brothers and sisters of mongol children. *Journal of Child Psychology and Psychiatry*, Vol. 15, 187–198.

Gath, A. (1977). The impact of an abnormal child upon the parents. *British Journal of Psychiatry*, 130, 405–410.

Gath, A. (1977). The effects of mental subnormality on the family. British *Journal of Psychiatry, Special Publication*, No. 9, 405–410.

Geismar, L.L. and Ayres, B. (1959, A method for evaluating the social functioning of families under treatment. *Social work*, 4, 102–108.

Geismar, L.L. (1962). Measuring family disorganisation. Marriage and Family Living, 24, 50–56.

Geismar, L.L. (1964). Family functioning as an index of need for welfare services. *Family Process*, 3, 99–113.

German, M.L. and Maisto, A.A. (1982). The relationship of a perceived family support system to the institutional placement of mentally retarded children. *Education and Training of Mentally Retarded*, 17, 17–23.

Gerson, D. (1967). Patterns of social functioning in families with marital and parent-child problems. University of Toronto Press.

Giband Wallston, J. and Wandersman, L.P. (1978). Development of utility of the parenting sense of competency scale. Paper presented at the Meeting of the American Psychological Association, Toronto.

Girimaji, R.S.C. (1993). Family intervention in mental retardation— An overview. *NIMHANS Journal*, 11 (1) Jan. 21–26.

Goffman, E. (1963). Stigma. Englewood Cliffs, N.J. Prentice Hall.

Goldber, S., Marcovitch, S. MacGregor, D. and Lojksek, M. (1986). Family responses to developmentally delayed pre-schoolers : Etiology and father's role. *American Journal of Mental Deficiency*, Vol. 96, No. 6, 610–617.

Goldenber, I. and Goldenberg, M. (1980). Family therapy : An overview. Monterey C.A. Brooks, Cole Publishing Co.

Goldie, L. (1966). Developmental medicine. *Child Neurology*, 8, 456.

Goldman, H.H. (1962). Mental illness and family bruden : A public health prospective. *Hospital and Community Psychiatry*, Vol. 33, 557–560.

Gordon, N.G., Dominque, D.P., Scigfried, M. and Deignam, L. (1982). Behavioural and emotional problems in mentally retarded youth. *Psychological Reports*, 5(1), 143–146.

Graliker, B., Koch, R. and Henderson, R. (1962). A study of factors influencing palcement of retarded children in a state residential institution. *American Journal of Mental Deficiency*, 66, 838–842.

Gumz, E.J. and Gubrium, J.F. (1972). Parental Perceptions of Mentally Retarded Children. *American Journal of Mental Retardation*, 77(2), 175.

Gupta, S.C. and Sethi, B.B. (1970). Prevalence of mental retardation in Uttar Pradesh. *Indian Journal of Psychiatry*, 12, 264.

Haldy, M.B. and Hanzlik, J.R. (1990). A comparison of perceived competence in child rearing between mothers of children with Down's Syndrome and mothers of children without delays. *Education and Training in Mental Retardation*, (June), 132–141.

Hammer, S. and Barnard, K. (1966). The mentally retarded adolescent. *Paediatrics*, 38(5), 845–857.

Hammer, M. (1983). "Core" and "Extended" social networks in relation to health and illness. *Social Science and Medicine*, 17, 405–411.

Harris, V.S. and McHale, S.M. (1989). Family life problems, daily care giving activities and the psycholgical well-being of mothers of mentally retarded children. *American Journal of Mental Retardation*, Vol. 94, No. 3, 231–239.

Heighway, S.M. Kiddwebster, S. and Snod, G.P. (1988). Supporting parents with mental retardation. *Children To-day*, 17(6) Nov. –Dec., 24–27.

Hill, R. (1949). *Families under stress.* New York : Harper and Row.

Hill, R. (1958). Genetic features of families under stress. Social Case Work, 49, 139–150.

Hodapp, R.M. and Zigler, E. (1993). Commentaries on Bierenbaum and Cohen. *Mental Retardation*, Vol. 31, No. 2, 75–77.

Holroyd, J. (1974). The Questionnaire on resources and stress : An instrument to measure family response to a handicapped member. *Journal of Community Psychology*, 2, 92–94.

Hot, K.S. (1958). The home care of severely mentally retarded.

Paediatrics, 22, 744–755.

Howard, J. (1978). The influence of children's developmental dysfunctions on marital quality and family interaction. In Lerner R.M. & Spanier, G.B. (Ed.), child influences on marital and family in interaction—A life span perspective, Academic Press, Inc. 275–297.

Hurcat, P.C. (1990). New dimensions in causes and cures in childhood disabilities. *Indian Journal of Disability and Rehabilitation*, Jan.–June, 69–74.

Hurder, W.P. (1973). The present situation and trends of research in the field of special education. UNESCO Report, Paris.

Illango, P.. and Nirmala, V. (1992). Burden of care of chronic mental illness. *The Indian Journal of Social Work*, Vol. L III, No. 1, 23–28.

Ingstad, B. and Sommerchild, H. (1983). Familien med ted funksjonshaemmede barnet. forlop-reaksjoner-mestring. Grupp Helsetjenesteforskning, rapport nr. 9 (English summary).

Ishtiag and Kamal. (1981). Sociological aspects of mental retardation. *Indian Journal of Mental Retardation.*

Jackson, D.D. (1959). Family interaction, family homeostasis and some implications for conjoint family psychotheraphy in individual and familial dynamics (Ed), J. Masserman–Grune and Stratton, New York.

Jain, M.C. Styavathy, K.' (1969). A preliminary note on the problems in the families with a mentally retarded child. Transactions of All India Institute of Mental Health, 9, 23–29.

Johnson, J.H. and Sarason, I.G. (1978). Life stress, depression and anxiety : Internal-external control as a moderator variable. *Journal of Psycho-somatic Research*, 22, 205–208.

Jones, R.R., Reid, J.B. and Patterson, G.R. (1975). Naturalistic observations in a clinical assessment. In P. Mc Reynolds (Ed), *Advances in Psychological Assessment*, Vol. 3, Sanfrancisco : Jossey-Bass.

Kaplan, D. (1978). Predicting the impact of severe illness in families. *Health and Social Work*, 1 (No. 3), 72–82.

Kaur, K. (1977). Coping with mentally retarded. *Journal of Social Welfare*, 23, 10.

Kazak, A.E. and Marvin, R.S. (1984). Differences, difficulties and adaptation : Stress and social net works in families with handicapped child. *Family Relations*, 33, 67–77.

Kershner, J.R. (1970). Studies in the psychological foundations of exceptionality (Ed) by Dissinger J.K. and Arnold, C.R. Brookscob Publishing Company. *Monterey*, C.A. 67–73.

Kogan, K.L., Wimberger, H.C. and Bobbitt, R.A. (1969). Analysis mother child interaction in young mental retardies. *Child Development*, 40, 799–812.

Kogan, K.L., Tyler, N. and Turner, P. (1974). The process of interpersonal adaptation between mothers and their cerebral palsied children. *Developmental Medicine and Child Neurology*, 16, 518–527.

Kogan, K.L., (1980). Interaction systems between pre-school handicapped or developmentally delayed children and their parents. In T.M., Field, S. Goldber, D. Stern and A.M. Sostek (Eds), High-Risk Infants and Children : Adult and Peer Interactions. New York : Academic Press.

Koller, H., Richardson, S.A., Katz, M. and Mclaren, J. (1983). Behaviour disturbance since childhood among a five year birth cohort of all mentally retarded young adults in a city. *American Journal of Mental Deficiency*, 87, (4, 386).

Koller, H., Richardson, S.A. and Katz, M. (1992). Families of children with mental retardation : Comprehensive view from an epidemiologic perspective. *American Journal on Mental Retardation*, Vol. 97, No. 3, 315–332.

Kothari C.R. (1985). Research Methodology—Methods and Techniques, Wiley Eastern Ltd., Delhi.

Krauss, M.W. (1993). Child related and parenting stress : Similarities and differences between mothers and fathers of children with disabilities. *American Journal on Mental Retardation*, Vol. 97, No. 4, 393–404.

Kravetz, S., Nativitz, R. and Katz, S. (1993). Parental coping styles and school adjustment of the children who are mentally retarded. *The British Journal of Developmental Disabilities*, Vol. XXXIX, No. 76, 51–59.

Krishnaswamy, J. (1992). Action Aid Disability News, Vol. 3, No. 2.

Kuppuswamy, B. (1968). A survey of mental retardation among children enrolled in middle schools of Mysore city. *Indian Journal of Mental Retardation*, 1, 12.

Lavee, Y., McCubbin, H.I. and Patterson, J.M. (1985). The double ABCX model of family stress and adaptation : An empirical test by analysis of structural equations with latent variables. *Journal of Marriage and Family*, Vol. 47, No. 4, 811–825.

Lesis, J.M. (1976). No single thread. Brunner/Mazel, New York.

Leyser, Y. and Dekel, G. (1990). Perceived stres and adjustment in religious jewish families with a child who is disabled. *The Journal of Psychology*, 125 (4), 427–438.

Locke, H.J. and Wallace, K.M. (1959). Short marital adjustment and predictive tests : Their relaibility and validity. *Marriage and Family Living*, August, 251–255.

Long, C.G. and Moore, J.R. (1979). Parental expectations for their epileptic children. *Journal of Child Psychology and Psychiatry*, 20, 299–312.

Lynn, McDonald, and Wikler, L. (1986). Periodic stresses of families of older mentally retarded children : An exploratory study. *American Journal of Mental Deficiency*, Vol. 90, No. 6, 703–706.

Madhavan, T., Narayan, J. and Suryaprakasam, B. (1991). Expectations of parents of their mentally retarded children. *The Andhra Pradesh Journal of Psychological Medicine*, Vol. 4, No. 2, 28–39.

Madhavan, T. and Narayan, J. (1992). Impact of intervention on the parental perceptions and expectations of their mentally retarded children. *Indian Journal of Social Work*, Vol. L III, No. 2, 191–201.

Malin, A.J. (1979). Malin's intelligence scale for indian children. Nagpur Child Guidance Centre, Nagpur.

Marshall, N.R. Hegrenes, J.R. and Goldstein, S. (1973). Verbal interactions : Mothers and their retarded children vz. mothers and their normal children. *American Journal of Mental Deficiency*, 77, 415–419.

Mash, E.J. and Johnston, C. (1983). Parental perceptions of child behaviour problems, parenting self-esteem and mother's reported stress in younger and older, hyperactive and normal children. *Journal of Consulting and Clinical Psychology*, 51, 86–99.

Mathur, S. and Nalwa, V. (1987). Misconceptions about mental retardation. *Indian Journal of Clinical Psychology*, Vol. 14, 19–21.

McAllister, R., Butler, E. and Lei, T.J. (1973). Patterns of social interaction among families of behaviourally retarded children. *Journal of Marriage and the Family*, 35, 93–100.

Mc Andrew, I. (1976). Children with a handicap and their families. Child Care, Health and Development, 2, 213–227.

McConachie, H. (1982). Fathers of mentally handicapped children in : Beail and J. Mcguire (Eds) : *Psychological aspects of Fatherhood*, 144–173. London : Junction.

McConachie, H. (1989). Mothers and fathers interaction with their young mentally handicapped children. *International Journal of Behavioural Development*, 12, 239–255.

McConachie, H.R. (1991). Home based teaching : What are we asking of parents ? *Child Care, Health and Development*, 17, 123–136.

McCubbin, H., Joy, C., Cauble, A.E., Comean, J., Patterson J.M., and Needle, R. (1980). Family stress and coping : A decade review. *Journal of Marriage and Family*, 42, 855–871.

McCubbin, H. and Patterson, J.M. (1982). Family stress and adaptation to crisis. A double ABCX model of family behaviour in D. Olson and B. Miller (Eds.). *Family Studies Review, Year Book*, 87–107. Baverly Hills, C.A. Sage.

McCubbin, H. and Patterson, J.M. (1983). Family stress. Adaptation to crisis. A double ABCS model of family behaviours. In H. McCubbin, M. Sussman and J. Patterson (Eds), social stresses and the family. Advances and Development in Family stress theory and Research, 7–37. New York : Howorth Press.

McDowell, J. and Gabel, H. (1981). Social support among mothers of retarded infants. Unpublished manuscript, George Peabody College, Nashvile.

McHale, S.M., Sloan, J. and Simeonsson, R.J. (1986). Sibling relationships of children with autistic, mentally retarded, and non-handicapped brothers and sisters. *Journal of Autism and Developmental disorders*, 16, 399–413.

Menolascino, F.J. (1972). Challenges in mental retardation : Progressive ideology and services, New York, Human Sciences Press.

Menolsascino, F.L. (1968). Parents of the mentally retarded : An operational approach to diagnosis and management. *Journal of the American Academy of Child Psychiatry*, 7, 589–602.

Menolascino, F.L. and Swansen, D.A. (1982). Emotional disorder in the mentally retarded. *British Journal of Mental Subnormality*, 28 (1, 54).

Meyer, R.J. (1980). Attitudes of parents of instituionalised mentally retarded individuals towards deinstitutionalisation. *American Journal of Mental Deficiency*, 85(2), 184–187.

Meyer, R.J. (1986). Fathers of handicapped children. In R.R. Fewell and P.F. Vadasy (Eds) families of handicapped children, needs and supports across the life span, 35–73, Austin Tx. Pro-Ed.

Mia, A., Islam, M.H. and Ali, M.A. (1979). Situation of physically handicapped children in Bangladesh. *A Field Survey*, Dhaka, Bangla, UNICEF.

Michael Bayley. "Mental Handicap and communty care" A study of mentally handicapped people in Sheffield. Routledge and Kegan Paul.

Miles, M. (1992). *Action Aid Disability News*, Vol. 3, No. 2.

Miller, B.C., Rollins, B.C. and Thomas, D.L. (1982). On methods of studying marriages and families. *Journal of Marriage and Family*, 44, 851–873.

Miller, W.H. and Keirn, W.C. (1978). Personality measurement in parents of retarded and emotionally disturbed children : A replication. *Journal of Clinical Psychology*, 34, 686–690.

Mink, I.T., Nihira, K. and Meyers, C.E. (1983). Taxonomy of family life styles : I. Homes with TMR children. *American Journal of Mental Deficiency*, Vol. 87, No. 5, 484–497.

Mink, I.T., Blacher, J. and Nihira, K. (1988). Taxonomy of family life styles : III replication with families with severely mentally retarded children. *American Journal on Mental Retardation*, Vol. 93, No. 3, 252–264.

Mink, I. T., (1993). In the best interests of the family : Some comments on Birenbaum'and Cohen's recommendations. Mental Retardation, April. Vol. 31, No. 2, 83–88.

Minnes, P.M. (1988). Family resources and stress associated with having a mentally retarded child. *American Journal on Mental Retardation*, Vol. 93, No. 2, 184–192.

Moos, R.H. and Moos, B.S. (1976). A typology of family social environments. *Family Process*, 15, 357–370.

Morney, R.M. (1981). Public social policy–impact on families with handicapped children. In : J.L. Paul (Ed) understanding and working with parents with special needs. New York : Hort, Rinehart and Winston.

Moudgil, A.C., Kumar, H. and Sharma, S. (1985). Buffering effect of social, emotional support on the parents of mentally retarded children. *Indian Journal of Clinical Psychology*, II, 63–70.

Narayanan, H.S. (1978). Impact of mentally retarded children on their families. M.D. Thesis, *NIMHANS*, Bangalore University.

Nihira, K. Meyers, C.E. and Mink, I.T. (1980). Home environment, family adjustment and development of emntally retarded children. *Applied Research in Mental Retardation*, Vol. 1,

5–24.

Nihira, K., Meyers, C.E. and Mink, I.T. (1983). Reciprocal relationship between home environment and development of TMR adolescents. *American Journal of Mental Deficiency*, Vol. 88, No. 2, 139–149.

Nihira, K., Weisner, T.S. and Bernheimer, L.P. (1994). Ecocultural assessment, in families of children with developmental delays : Construct and concurrent validities. *American Journal on Mental Retardation*, Vol. 98, No. 5, 551–556.

Olshansky, S. (1962). Chronic Sorrow : A response to having a mentally defective child. *Social Case Work*, 43, 190–192.

Olson, D.H. (1979). Circumplex model of marital and family systems : Cohesion and adaptability dimension, family types, clinical application. *Family Process*, 18 (March), 3–27.

Orr, R.R., Cameron, S.J. and Day, D.M. (1991). Coping with stress in family with children who have mental retardation : An evaluation of the double ABCX model. *American Journal on Mental Retardation*, Vol. 95, No. 4, 444–450.

Orr, R.R. Cameron, S.J., Dobson, L.A. and Day, D.M. (1993). Age related changes in stress experienced by families with a child who has developmental delays. *Mental Retardation*, Vol. 31, No. 3, 171–176.

Otto, H.A. (1963). Criteria for assessing family strength. *Family Process*, 2 (No. 2), 329–337.

Pai, S. and Kapur, R.L. (1981). The burden of a family of a psychiatric patient : Development of an interview schedule. *British Journal of Psychiatry*, 138, 332–335.

Parke, R. (1988). Foreword in P. Bronstein and C. Covan (Eds) fatherhood today : Men's changing role in the family. (Pp IX–XII). New York : Willey.

Patterson, G.R. (1976). The aggressive child : victim and architect of a coercive system. In E.J. Mash, L.A. Hamerlynck and L.C. Handy (Eds). Behaviour Modification and Families. New York : Bruner/Mazel.

Patterson, G.R. (1980). Mothers : The un-acknowledged victims. Monographs of the Society for Research in Child Development, 45 (5, Serial No. 186).

Pelz, S.L., Levy, S., Tamir, A., Spenser, T. and Epstein, L.M. (1984). A measure of family functioning for health care practice and research in Israel. *Journal of Comparative Family Studies*, Vol. XV, No. 2. 211–230.

Peshawaria, R., Venkatesan, S. and Menon, D.K. (1988). Consumer demand of services by parents of mentally handicapped individuals. *Indian Journal of Disability and Rehabilitation*, July–Dec., 48–57.

Peshawaria, R., and Menon, D.K. (1989). Parent involvement in the training and management of their mentally handicapped persons. *Journal of Personality and Clinical Studies*, 5, 2, 217–221.

Peshawaria, R., Venkatesan, S. and Menon, D.K. (1990). Behaviour problems in mentally handicapped persons : An analysis of parent needs. *Indian Journal of Clinical Psychology*, Vol. 17, No. 2, 63–70.

Peshawaria, R., Venkatesan, S., Mahapatra, B. and Menon, D.K. (1990). Teachers' perceptions of problem behaviours among mentally handicapped persons in special school settings. *Indian Journal of Disability and Rehabilitation*, Jan.–June, 23–29.

Peshawaria, R., Reddi, V.S., Subbarao, T.A. and Persha, A.J. (1991). Group parent training programmes as NIMH : An overview. *Journal of Personality Clinical Studies*, 7, 169–174.

Peshawaria, R. and Menon, D.K. (1992). Working with families of children with mental handicap in India : Various Models.

Prabhu, C.G. (1968). The participation of the parents in the services for the retarded. *Indian Journal of Mental Retardation*, Vol. 1, No. 1, 4–11.

Prabhu, C.G., Varma, N., John, A., Daniel, E. and Elizebeth, C.K. (1985). Mental retardation in India. In : G.G. Prabhu (Ed), Souvenir of the 7th World Congress of the International Association for the Scientific Study of Mental Deficiency, New

Delhi, India, March, 24–28.

Pratt, L. (1976). Family structure and effective health behaviour : The energised family. Houghton Miffin, Boston.

Puri, M. and Sen, A.K. (1989). Mentally retarded children in India. Mittal Publications, New Delhi, No. 110059, India, 79–85.

Purnima, N.M. (1990). Coping with the developmentally delayed child : The trials and tribulations of parents. *The Indian Journal of Social-work*, Vol. LI, No. 4, 553–566.

Ramadevi, M. (1991). Attitudes of rural children towards their mentally retarded siblings. Unpublished Dissertation submitted for Master's degree, Sri Venkateswara University.

Ramagopal, C.N. and Madhu Rao. (1994). A study of behaviour disorders in moderately mentally retarded children and their relation to parental attitude. *Indian Journal of Clinical Psychology*, Vol. 21, (2) Sep, 27–31.

Reed, E.W. and Reed, S.C. (1965). Mental retardation : A family study. Philadelphia : Saunders.

Reiss, D. (1981). The family's construction of reality. Harvard University Press, Cambride, M.A.

Reiss, S. (1982). Psycho-pathology and mental retardation : Survey of developmental disabilities, mental health programme. *Mental Retardation*, 20, 128–132.

Report, (1989). Rural camps as an enabling approach to the rehabilitation of the mentally handicapped. Thakur Hari Prasad Insitutue of Research and Rehabilitation for the Mentally Handicapped, Hyderabad.

Richards, I.D.G., and McIntosh, H.T. (1973). Spin bifida survivors and their parents : A study of problems and services. Developmental Medicine and Neurology. 15, 293.

Richardson, S.A., Koller, H. and Katz, M. (1985). Relationship of up-bringing to later behaviour disturbance of mildly mentally retarded young people. *American Journal of Mental Deficiency*, Vol. 90, No. 1, 1–8.

Roghmann, K.J. (1973). Family coping with every day illness : Self reports from household survey. *Journal of Cmparative Family* Studies, 4 (No. 1), 49–62.

Ross. (1964). The exceptional child in the family. Helping parents of exceptional children, 64–67. New York : Grune and Stratton.

Rousey, A.M., Best, S.A., and Blacher, J. (1992). Mothers' and fathers' perceptions of stress and coping with children who have severe disabilities. *American Journal on Mental Retardation*, Vol. 97, No. 1, 99–109.

Rowitz, L. (1992). A family affair : *Mental Retardation*, 30 (2), iii-iv.

Rutter, M. (1970). Sex differences in children's responses to family stress. In the child in his family. (Edited by Anthony, E.J. and Koupernik, C.). International Year Book for Child Psychiatry. Wiley Inter Science, London.

Sabbeth, B.F. and Leventhal, J.M. (1984). Marital adjustment to chronic childhood illness : A critique of the Literature. Paediatrics, 73, 762–768.

Saetermoe, C.L., Widaman, K.F. and Duffy, S.B. (1991). Validation of the parenting style. Survey for parents of children with mental retardation. *Mental Retardation*, No. 3, 149–157.

Schonell, F.J. and Watts, B.J. (1957). A first survey of the effects of a subnormal child on the family unit. *American Journal of Mental Deficiency*, 61, 210–219.

Sell, H.L. (1984). Caring for the mentally retarded in developing countries. *International Journal of Mental Health*, 12(3), 58–76.

Seltzer, M.M. and Krauss, M.W. (1989). Aging parents with adult mentally retarded children : Family risk factors and sources of support. *American Journal on Mental Retardation*, Vol. 94, No. 3, 303–312.

Sen, A. (1988). Prevalence of mental retardation in rural indian and some of its psycho-social concomitants. *Indian Journal of Rehabilitation Research*, Vol. 11, No. 3, 290–293.

Sequeira, E.M., Madhu Rao, P., Subbakrishna, D.K. and Prabhu, C.G. (1990). Perceived burden and coping styles of the mothers of mentally handicapped children. *NIMHANS Journal*, 8(1), Jan., 63–67.

Seshadri, M., Verma, V.K., Verma, S.K. and Pershad, D. (1983). Impact of a mentally handicapped child on the family. *Indian Journal of Clinical Psychology*, 10, 473–478.

Seth, S. (1979). Maternal attitude towards mentally retarded children. In : E.G. Parameswaran and S. Bhogle (Ed), *Developmental psychology*, New Delhi, Light and Life Publishers.

Sethi, B.B. and Sitholey, P. (1986). A study of the time utilisation, perception of burden and help expectation of mothers of urban mentally retarded children. *Indian Journal of Social Psychiatry*, 2, 25–44.

Shah, G. (1989). Working with parents of handicapped children. *The Indian Journal of Social Work*, Vol. L, No. 4, 483–495.

Shulman, S., Margalit, M., Gadish, O. and Stuchiner, N. (1990). The family system of moderately mentally retarded children. *Journal of Mental Deficiency Research*, 34, 341–350.

Silver, R.L. and Wortman, C.B. (1980). "Coping with undersirable life events". Pp. 279–375 in J. Garber and M.E.P. Seligman (Eds), *Human Helplessness*. New York : Academic Press.

Singer, G.H.S., Irvin, L.K. and Hawkins, N. (1988). Stress management training for parents of children with severe handicaps. *Mental Retardation*, Vol. 26, No. 5, 269–277.

Singh, M.V. and Dager, B. (1982). Sociological aspects of behaviour problems in a community child guidance centre. *Child Psychiatry Quarterly*, 15(2), 43–49.

Skrtic, T.M., Summers, J.A., Brotherson, M.J. and Turnbull, A.P. (1984). Severely handicapped children and their brothers and sisters, In J. Blacher (Ed). young severely handicapped children and their families : Research in review. New York : Academic Press.

Smilkstein, G. (1978). The family AGPAR : A proposal for a family function test and its use by physicians. *Journal of Family*

Practices, 6, 1231–1239.

Solnit, A. and Stark, M.H. (1961). Mourning the birth of a defective child. *Psycho-Analytic Study of the Child*, 16, 523.

Srinivasa Murthy, R., Wig, N.N. and Dhir, A. (1980). Rural community attitude to mental retardation. *Child Psychiatry Quarterly*, Vol. XIII, No. 1, 81–88.

Srivastava, R.V., Saxena, V. and Saxena, N.K. (1975). Attitude of mothers of mentally retarded children towards certain aspects of child-rearing practices. *Indian Journal of Mental Retardation*, 9, 77–82.

Stanton, M.D. (1981). Marital therapy from a structural/strategic view point. In Sholevar, G.P. (Ed), Marriage is a family affair : A text book of marriage and marital therapy. New York : NY SP Medical and Scientific Books.

Stoneman, Z. (1989). Comparison Groups in research on families with mentally retarded members. A methodological and conceptual review. *American Journal on Mental Retardation*, Vol. 94, No. 3, 195–215.

Stoneman, Z. and Crapps, J.M. (1990). Mentally retarded individuals in family care homes : Relationships with the family of origin. American *Journal on Mental Retardation*, Vol. 94, No. 4, 420–430.

Suelzle, M. and Keenan, V. (1981). Changes in family support networks over the life cycle of mentally retarded persons. *American Journal of Mental Deficiency*, 86, 267–274.

Swain, J. and Eagle, P. (1987). The views of parents and carers : working with others. *Mental Handicap*, Vol. 15, 152–154.

Tallman, I. (1965). Spousal role differentiation and the socialisation of severely retarded children. *Journal of Marriage and Family*, 37–42.

Tangri, P. and Verma, P. (1992). A study of social burden felt by mothers of handicapped children. *Journal of Personality and Clinical Studies*, 8(2), 117–120.

Terdal, L.E., Jackson, R.H. and Garner, A.M. (1976). Mother child interactions. A comparison between normal and developmentally delayed groups—In E.J. Mash, L.A. Hammerlynck and L.C. Handy. (Eds). Behaviour modification and families. New York : Brunner/Mazel.

Twe, B.J., Payne, H., Lawrence, K.M. (1974). Must a family with handicapped member be a handicapped family ? *Developmental Medicine and Child Neurology*, 16, (Pp. 32), 95–98.

Thressiakutty, A.T. and Narayan, J. (1990). Parental perceptions of problems and expectations regarding their mentally retarded children. *Indian Journal of Disablity and Rehabilitation*, 4, 59–63.

Tilam, D. (1994). Community integration of mentally handicapped persons. *The Indian Journal of Social Work*, Vol. LV, No. 1, 48–59.

Tizard, J. and Grad, J.C. (1961). The mentally handicapped and their families—A social survey, maudsley monograph 7. London : Oxford Unviersity Press.

Tucker, M.B. (1982). Social support and coping : Applications for the study of female drug abuse. *Journal of Social Issues*, 38(2), 117–137.

Tung, S. and Jagijit. (1994). Sex differences on a measure of coping strategies. *Journal of Psychological Researches*, Vol. 38, No. 1 & 2, 10–13.

Turnbull, A.P., Summers, J.A. and Bortherson, M.J. (1983). Family life cycle. Theoretical and empirical implications and future directions for families with mentally retarded members. Paper presented at the NICHD conference on families with retarded children. Rougemont, N.C.

Turnbull, A.P., Summer, J.A. and Brotherson, M.J. (1983). Working with families with disabled members. A family systems perspective. Lawrence, K.S. University of Kausas. Research and Training Centre on independent living.

Udai Pareek. and Venkateswara Rao, T. (1992). First handbook of psychological and social instrument, 310–311. New Delhi : Concept Publishing Co.

Veena, S.G. (1985). Management problems and practices of homemakers with a disabled member in the family. *The Indian Journal of Social Work*, Vol. XLV, No. 4, (Jan.).

Venkatesan, S., and Das, A.K. (1994). Reported burden on family members in receiving/implementing home based training programmes for children with mental handicaps. *Journal of Psychological Researches*, Vol. 38, No. 1 and 2, 39–45.

Verma, V.K., Verma, S.K., and Kapoor, P. (1992). Evaluation of home care programme for the metnally retarded children through training of the mother. *Indian Journal of Medical Research*, Vol. 96, 29–36.

Vickie, S., Harris. and Susan M. McHale (1989). Family life problems, daily coregiving activities and the psychological well-being of mothers of mentally retarded children. *American Journal on Mental Retardation*, Vol. 94, No. 3, 231–239.

Vijayalakshmi, B., and Ramana, K.V., (1987). Use of culture specific coping structures by families of mentally ill patients. *The Indian Journal of Social Work*, Vol. XLVIII, No. 2, 163–169.

Vitze, P.M., Abernathy, S.R., Ashe, M.L. and Faulstich, G. (1978). Contingency interaction between mothers and their developmentally delayed infants. In G.P. Sackett (Ed), *Observing Behaviour* (Vol. I), Balitmore : University Park Press.

Voysey, A. (1975). A constant burden : the reconstruction of family life. Routledge and Kegan Paul, London.

Wahler, R.G. (1980). The insular mother : Her problems in parent child treatment. *Journal of Applied Behaviour Analysis*, 13, 207–219.

Waisbern, S.E. (1980). Parents reaction after the birth of a developmentally disabled child. *American Journal of Mental Deficiency*, 84, 345–351.

Walker, A.J. (1985). Reconceptualizing family stress. *Journal of Marriage and The Family*, Vol. 47, No. 4, 827–837.

Wallander, J.L. and Varni, J.W, (1989). Social support and adjustment in chronically ill and handicapped children. *American Journal of Community Psychology*, Vol. 17, No. 2, 185–201.

Wells, K. and Whittington, D. (1993). Child and family functioning after intensive family preservation services. *Social Service Review*, March, 55–83.

Wikler, L. (1981). Chronic stresses in families of mentally retarded children. *Family relations*, 30, 281–288.

Wikler, L., Wasoki, K. and Hatfield, E. (1981). Chronic sorrow revisited parent vz. professional depiction of the adjustment of parents of mentally retarded children. *American Journal of Orthopsychiatry*, 51, 63–70.

Wikler, L.M. (1986). Periodic stresses of families of older mentally retarded children. A Exploratory Study, *American Journal of Mental Deficiency*, Vol. 90, No. 6, 703–706.

Wilkin, D. (1979). Caring for the mentally handicapped child. Lond Croomhelm.

Wilton, K. and Renaut, J. (1986). Stress levels in families with intellectually handicapped pre-school children and families with non-handicapped pre-school children. *Journal of Mental Deficiency Research*, 30, 163–169.

Wishart, M.C., Bidder, R.J. and Gray, O.P. (1980). Parental responses to their developmentally delayed child. *Child-Care, Health and Development*, 7, 267–279.

Wolfensberger, W. (1967). Counselling parents of the retarded. In Baumeister, A.A. (Ed). mental retardation : Education, appraisal and research. Chicago : Aldine Publishing Co.

Wolfensberger, W. (1968). Counselling the parents of the retarded. In A.A. Baumeister (Ed.), Mental Retardation : Appraisal, education and rehabilitation. Chicago : Aldine.

Wolfensberger, W. (1970). The principle of normalisation and its implications in psychiatric services. *American Journal of Psychiatry*, 127, 291–297.

Wolfensberger, W. (1972). Normalisation. National Institute of Mental Retardation, Canada.

Yungchen, C. (1980). A preliminary study of the family AGPAR index. *Acta Paediatrica Sinica*, 21, (No. 3), 210–217.

Zuk, G.H. (1959). Religious factor and the role of guilt in parents acceptance of the retarded child. *American Journal of Mental Deficiency*, 64, 130.

Zuk, G.H., Miller, R.I., Bartram, J.B., and Kling, F. (1962). Maternal acceptance of retarded children : A questionnaire study of attitudes and religious background. *Child-development*, 32, 515–540.